The Texas Experience

The Texas Experience

Compiled by
Archie P. McDonald

PUBLISHED FOR
The Texas Committee for the Humanities
BY
Texas A&M University Press
COLLEGE STATION

Library of Congress Cataloging-in-Publication Data

McDonald, Archie P.
   The Texas experience.

   1. Texas—History.   I. Texas Committee for the
Humanities.   II. Title.
F386.M346   1986   976.4   85-40755
ISBN 0-89096-281-2

Manufactured in the United States of America
First Edition

Contents

Foreword

An exceptional history, enriched by folklore and literature, has given Texans a distinctive identity. Their work and play, their struggles and celebrations shine through our historical presentation, the Texas Experience.

The commerce and agriculture that characterize Texas today extend back centuries, to the time when Caddo Indians developed a farming and trading empire in the Neches Valley. In the nineteenth century, Texas became a contested land, where Spanish soldiers and friars tried to push New Spain's frontier northward and Anglo-American colonists sought to maintain independence beyond the U.S. border. Hispanic and Anglo contact has continued to contribute to the spirit that has distinguished Texas, as has its experience as the only American state to have been an independent republic years before acquiring statehood.

From Hispanic, black, and Anglo vaqueros to immigrant German artists and contemporary musicians, from early leaders like President Sam Houston and San Antonio mayor Juan Sequín to later reformers like Governor James Hogg and President Lyndon B. Johnson, Texans have shown a venturous determination. Vast land and enterprising citizens have made Texas excel in agriculture, ranching, petroleum, computers, and many other ventures.

The celebration of the sesquicentennial commemorating the founding of the Texas Republic offered an exciting opportunity to examine our state's remarkable history and culture. Amid all the hoopla and crass commercialism of this celebration, it seemed imperative that we devote some effort to reflecting on our roots—the cultural and historical heritage that gives identity to us as individuals and as a people. That is precisely what this book attempts to do. However, it is not an exercise in antiquarianism, glorifying the past or simply presenting it for its own sake. Studying the past can have important implications for the present and the future as well. An understanding of one's history, literature, and folklore—in short, of the core fields of the humanities—reveals the events and values that have defined and shaped us and that continue to influence our beliefs and actions. Such an understanding can help unite all Texans, native and naturalized alike, as we plan and move into the future together.

Our approach in this book is chronological, moving from the earliest peoples to present-day Texans; topical, emphasizing key events that affected generations of Texans—not just the famous but ordinary people, too; and multidisciplinary. The multidisciplinary approach should make the book appealing to both native Texans and newcomers, in that it presents both traditional history and relatively fresh intellectual material and perspectives. For example, while we cover important military and political events, such as the Battle of the Alamo, we have also included aspects of social, ethnic, and women's history as well as archaeology, literature, folklore, American studies, and so forth.

The latter fields open up the domain of Texas mythology, which we also attempt to interpret along with the historical events. Texas myths — the figures and stories that convey values and give meaning to our lives — can be found in works of popular culture, especially novels, film, and television shows. From the cowboy and wildcatter heroes of stage and screen to the television series "Dallas," Texas has continued to inspire a rich stock of mythological stories and figures that have influenced not only the state's character but also the national character. Although such Texan writers as J. Frank Dobie and Walter Prescott Webb have had a hand in advancing the Western version of the Texas myth, other regions, especially Hollywood, have appropriated and manipulated these stereotypical images. Transcending the state's boundaries, the mythical Texan has reflected and influenced national cultural values.

In the process of sorting out the mythical elements from the historical ones and interpreting them according to methods appropriate to each, we hope to erase certain stereotypical views of Texas, which, if not completely inaccurate, certainly distort the reality of the state. Above all, the stereotypical Texan, the Western cowboy, is fixed in many people's minds as the typical Texan in reality and historical fact. This confusion masks not only the earlier Southern roots of our state, but also its rich ethnic diversity. At last count the Institute of Texan Cultures had identified thirty ethnic groups that have contributed to our heritage.

Closely related to this cultural diversity is immigration. In my view, we cannot tell the story of Texas without focusing on the continuous waves of immigrants that have come to this region at one time or another: from the Paleo-Indians to the Spanish conquistadors and missionaries, from the Comanches to the Anglo-American settlers and black captives, from the late nineteenth-century Central and Eastern European ethnic groups to the more recent newcomers from other states, Mexico, and the Far East. Immigration and ethnicity are recurring themes in the Texas experience.

The variety of topics covered in this book are presented as vignettes, independent of one another for the most part. Each vignette reveals a tidbit of the subtleties and complexities of the state's remarkable history. Just as the individual pieces of a quilt, when sewn together, form a unified pattern, so too these independent vignettes taken together present a broad picture of the state's history. The book, however, is not meant to be comprehensive, either in the sense of treating each topic definitively or in the sense of covering every aspect of the history of the state. Rather, it attempts to present some of the more important events that have influenced the development of the state. Each vignette concludes with a suggestion for further reading – or listening or viewing, where that is appropriate – for those whose appetites have been whetted.

The genesis of the book accounts for its vignette nature. The book represents the culmination of a major media program for the Sesquicentennial on the part of the Texas Committee for the Humanities, the state program of the National Endowment for the Humanities. In light of our mission to promote public humanities programs in Texas, it was fitting that the committee play a leadership role in this major public education endeavor. This media program consisted of statewide television and newspaper series on Texas history and culture – fifty-two one-minute spots for broadcast, one per week throughout 1986, complemented by a weekly newspaper series covering the same topic each week. The vignettes in this book are based on the background material, furnished by some fifty scholars, that informed that project.

Besides these scholars, many other Texans have made significant contributions to "The Texas Experience" at every stage of its development, including all three components: television spots, newspaper articles, and the book. An advisory committee consisting of both humanities scholars and media professionals nurtured the project through its gestation period, recommending topics and resource scholars. This committee involved the following scholars: historian Archie McDonald and folklorist Francis Abernethy of Stephen F. Austin State University, historian Elizabeth Enstam and English professor Marshall Terry of Southern Methodist University,

archaeologist Thomas Hester of the University of Texas at San Antonio, historian Oscar Martínez of the University of Texas at El Paso, historian Ben Procter of Texas Christian University, historian Ron Tyler of the Amon Carter Museum, and folklorist Melvin Wade of the University of Texas at Austin. Media consultants included Mary Francis Byrne and Frank O'Neil, general manager of KXAS-TV (NBC affiliate in Dallas–Fort Worth), and Bob Ray Saunders of KERA-TV (PBS affiliate in Dallas–Fort Worth). I also profited from frequent discussions with L. Tuffly Ellis and Tom Cutrer of the Texas State Historical Association.

KXAS-TV was responsible for the production of the television series. Doug Adams, news director of the station, served as the executive producer, while independent filmmaker Jim Ruddy of the Ruddy Group Inc. of Dallas handled the actual production. Marise McDermott, former editor of *The Texas Journal,* edited the newspaper articles. Sherilyn Brandenstein, my colleague at the Texas Committee for the Humanities, contributed to every phase of the project. In particular, she coordinated the newspaper series and tracked down visuals for the series and this book, with the assistance of Ron Stone, Jr., a graduate student at the University of Texas at Austin. Color photographs in this book come from *Texas Highways* magazine, with the cooperation of their staff.

Special thanks is due to our funding sources: The Shell Companies Foundation, Inc., of Houston, Doris J. O'Connor, senior vice-president; the Hoblitzelle Foundation of Dallas, Robert Lynn Harris, executive director; and the State Programs

Division of the National Endowment for
the Humanities. We also profited from the
encouragement and counsel of John Haines,
advertising manager at Shell Oil Company
and the key figure behind the highly successful 1976 Bicentennial Minutes, and his
colleagues at the Houston office of Ogilvy
and Mather, Kirk Walden and Joe Kilgore,
who perceptively critiqued our television
scripts and production design.

Although the Texas Sesquicentennial inspired this book, we designed it to have a
lifespan far beyond 1986, with the hope
that it will last long after the last Sesquicentennial trinket has faded from memory
— an enduring gift from the board members and staff of the Texas Committee for
the Humanities to the people of Texas.

Robert F. O'Connor
Project Director,
"The Texas Experience"

Preface

That time when none but the classicists knew what the word *Sesquicentennial* meant seems long ago. Now we Texans live, breathe, and eat with the word, even if some of us have not yet learned to say it easily. Its logo adorns virtually every official state letter or publication, and its flag flies over countless official Sesquicentennial communities and gives sanction to untold numbers of commemorative products. It is a great tourist attraction and the gaudiest show since at least the Centennial in 1936. In its course, some serious thought will have been given to where we have been and where we are going. A few books, such as this one, will have attempted to capture some sense of the state's development over the past 150 years of independence, as well as the influence of the earlier years.

While all about us souvenirs are hawked, a few to be preserved as antiques for the Bicentennial and Tercentennial inevitably to follow, it is appropriate for the Texas Committee for the Humanities (a state program of the National Endowment for the Humanities) to involve the scholarly community in a collective look at the state of the state. This effort has involved women and men, Anglos, Mexican Americans, blacks, and other interested groups. Our individual goals, each to examine one small slice of the state's history, have cul-

minated in the array of vignettes in this collective book.

The project began in 1983 when the Texas Committee for the Humanities requested grant proposals on the topic of Texas myths. This produced such an abundance of proposals and interest that the committee was encouraged to pursue the theme of Texas history during the Sesquicentennial with its own public programs. First came the idea of a Sesquicentennial Minutes series, to be made available to television markets around the state. Early in the process the committee decided that the scriptwriter should have access to the best scholarship available so that the television series could present accurate as well as interesting history. A committee of scholars representing various humanities fields selected a still larger group to write more than seventy essays on subjects as varied as Juneteenth, literary figures, and political crises. With these brief, two-page essays at hand, it became obvious that more could and should be done with them. Soon they were used as the background material for this book, and for a weekly newspaper series as well.

For this book, we took the information provided by the several scholars and edited it for publication. Sometimes this meant expanding a piece a bit to provide context; sometimes it meant adding a few examples. In doing this, I have drawn freely on my own previous research, including my textbook, *Texas: All Hail the Mighty State* (Austin: Eakin Press, 1983). I have tried to make the style uniform enough for easy reading, but the basic information comes from these experts in their fields.

The story of Texas that emerges from this collective effort necessarily is different from one that would result from the work of a single writer or even a smaller writing team. We do not all agree, for example, about the treatment and circumstance of Mexican Americans and their intermingled activities with Anglos in our state's history, about the considerable contribution of Texas women and the recognition of that contribution, or even about the causes and results of the Texas Revolution itself. But we all agree that these topics are important and that they should be studied and discussed.

For my part, it has been an enlightening experience. My colleagues have taught me a good deal about their specialties in our shared interest, particularly their interpretations. This is probably the most significant result of our labors for most of our readers as well. It offers an opportunity to see the state and its institutions from such varied perspectives as the traditional one shared by many in the Anglo community and the quite different ones held by many Texas minorities. Probably none of the perspectives is wholly correct; all have some truth in them for each of us to learn.

Finally, one of the principal messages of our work is that Texas is big enough, physically and culturally, for all of us. We have all come as immigrants. We have jostled

for centuries, especially for the last 150 years, for a sense of place. Not all of us are satisfied with the place that circumstance presently affords us, but a primal truth that emerges from a study such as this is that change is eternal. Our place may improve with our efforts and the good will of others, or it may decline if we are not vigilant. We can change ourselves and our institutions to earn the best possible place for us all that our environment affords. This, after all, is a proper function for the humanities: to learn from and about people and their environment; to study their interactions, their differences and agreements; and, ultimately, to appreciate them. It is our hope, and mine especially, that this work has contributed to that end.

Archie P. McDonald

The Texas
Experience

Texas' great variety of landforms fall into three principal geographic regions: the coastal prairie, the rolling plains, and the mountain zone, which includes desert. Map courtesy of Robin Doughty.

The Land

Texas was "a spot of earth almost unknown to the geography of the age," Sam Houston said in 1836. The state of Texas was then a hope, a political dream, an economic nightmare, a storehouse of precious energy awaiting an appropriate technology, and much more. But the land of Texas —most of it—remained pristine, the product more of geological and biological interactions than of human influence.

Long before anyone called this land Texas, 250 million years ago in the Pennsylvanian Age, mountains spanned the distance between the Red River and the Big Bend country. A shallow sea inundated the land to the northwest, and dry land lay to the south and east where the Gulf of Mexico is now. Then the earth heaved, the sea drained away from the north, and the dry land became a continental shelf, covered by new waters. Over long time the mountains eroded, and sediment cov-

3

ered the plant and animal life for future discoveries as fossil fuels. At last, less than 100 million years ago, further upheaval rearranged the land into about the form it holds today, making Texas a place of convergence for all the major landforms of North America: the southern forest, the central prairies, and the western mountains.

Thus it lay, relatively undisturbed by human intervention when Sam Houston made his comment in his inaugural address to the first congress of the Republic of Texas. Indians had known the land for several thousand years; for some two and a half centuries Spaniards (and after independence in 1820, Mexicans) had claimed it. But beyond its borders, few knew much of this Texas until Anglos began to migrate to Texas legally in the 1820s. In their reports, they classified the portion of it that concerned them most in three regions: the Coastal Prairie, the Rolling Prairie, and the "mountain" or western region.

The Coastal Prairie formed an arc along the Gulf of Mexico. Rising only a little above sealevel, it was filled with marshes, oak clumps or mottes, and black clay soils that became sandier and drier to the south. An exposed coastline of sprawling bays and sand dunes, which offered only a few safe harbors like Galveston, opened onto the flat, grass-filled plain of the Coastal Prairie. The region would gain fame among hunters as a "nation of geese." Whereas later visitors would throng to fashionable beaches to inhale the bracing air and seek health, at the time when Houston spoke to the Congress, the coastal zone was considered unhealthy. Malarial fevers and such pests as mosquitoes thrived in Galveston, Brazoria, Indianola, and other communities near the coast. Promoters often consequently advised immigrants to move to the more elevated region, known as the Rolling Prairies.

Commentators likened this land to classical Greece and Rome. Stretching north from the Sabine River to the Red River and west to the Balcones Escarpment, the Rolling Prairies offered a mild climate, fertile soils, abundant wood, pure water, and deer, turkey, and other game animals. People from Louisiana and Arkansas who settled in this region usually headed for Austin's Colony, converging on Nacogdoches, at one end of the old Spanish Royal Highway, the Camino Real. From there, they pushed westward through a region thick with hardwoods and loblolly and shortleaf pines. They forded many rivers along the way and passed through clearings that gradually increased in size as they moved west. The gently undulating land, which held both woodland and prairie, was ripe with promise for farmers, who felled trees for building materials and turned the sod for cotton, corn, and other staples. Today a part of this region, the Blackland Prairie, running from near San Antonio north through Austin, Waco, and Dallas, constitutes the largest acreage continuously in cultivation in the state. It is an area where change has been dramatic and the human imprint indelible.

Austin became the gateway to the remote and unexplored "mountain" or western region, which lay beyond the Colorado River. Foliage decreased with the decreasing rainfall as travelers passed through the rough limestone upland of the Edwards

Plateau. Beyond the Pecos River, they entered a true desert, where short range grasses, creosote bushes, and mesquite covered basins that received less than ten inches of moisture a year. Throngs of mustangs, bison, and pronghorn antelope roamed mountain Texas, and mule deer and bighorn sheep lived in the high uplands. It was a harsh environment, with drought and extremes of heat and cold.

The boundaries assigned the three regions of early Anglo Texas in emigrant literature from the 1830s on varied. It was not always obvious where one region ended and another began. The general distinctions writers made, however, helped settlers sort out the choices open to them. Usually guides and settlers alike preferred the second region—the middle ground, the focus of early settlement—where the natural "parkland" of wood and prairie offered enormous promise for crops.

Change is a characteristic of all environments, even those far removed from human activity, but the changes induced by settlement are of a different sort than those brought about by the action of wind, water, and geologic faulting. Rural settlement introduced substantial environmental change in Texas, increasing from the effects of nomadic Indian life through the ranch life of the Spanish period to the farming developed in later years, with stock tanks for cattle and goats, pastures, fences, and croplands. Urban life—with its dense habitation, replacement of native vegetation with ornamental shrubbery and concrete, and machine-altered grades—has changed the environment still more drastically. Modern Texas, consequently, is far different than the unmapped land Sam Houston and the early settlers knew. As various cultures have come to Texas, they have tapped natural resources, altered the distribution and abundance of native plants and animals, imported new ones, and carved a modern industrial society out of a vast, thinly settled, and little-known region.

☆ Information on the Anglo settlers' view of Texas geography was provided by Robin W. Doughty, associate professor of geography at the University of Texas at Austin. If you would like to learn more about these early views of Texas, check your local bookstore or library for Professor Doughty's book *Wildlife and Man in Texas: Environmental Change and Conservation* (College Station: Texas A&M University Press, 1983).

Paleo-Indians

It was cooler then and more moist; clusters of pine and fir dotted the landscape of what is now Texas. The glaciers and ice that had coated much of North America did not extend that far south, but Ice Age conditions were nonetheless far different than today's. Mammoths, large bison, horses, camels, and ground sloths roamed

5

By the Ice Age, Paleo-Indians were hunting massive bison with spear throwers, or atlatls, *tipped with small fluted points, but wild plants provided much of their staple food.* Illustration © by Hal M. Story for *The Indians of Texas: From Prehistoric to Modern Times* by W. W. Newcomb, Jr. (Austin: University of Texas Press, 1961). Courtesy of the Texas Memorial Museum, Austin.

the land, game for the first humans to arrive on that soil, the Paleo-Indians.

They had come, these earliest Native Americans, across the continent during the Pleistocene, or Ice Age. Wherever they lived or hunted, they left behind chipped flint projectile points and knives and the remains of animals they had killed and butchered. The distinctive forms of these projectile points are used to identify the cultures of prehistory.

The ancient people made their way

south to Texas perhaps as early as 9200 B.C. There at an important site near Miami, in Roberts County in the Texas Panhandle, they left distinctive fluted spear tips. These tips, used in hunting mammoths, are called Clovis spear tips, and the people who used them, including these first known Texans, are identified as the Clovis Complex.

Later Ice Age hunters sought the free-ranging bison—which, unlike their descendants, the buffalo, had long, straight horns. For this game they tipped their spears with smaller fluted points, known as Folsom points. At Bonfire Shelter, near Langtry on the Rio Grande in Val Verde County, Folsom hunters drove herds of bison over the edge of a steep canyon wall and butchered them in a sheltered area below. The remains of this slaughter, dating from around 8800–8500 B.C., provide evidence of the presence of these Ice Age hunters and give clues to their hunting methods. Folsom campsites have been found near San Antonio and Abilene and at Lubbock Lake in West Texas.

Paleo-Indians had to adapt to an environment more like that of today as the Ice Age slowly closed, around 8000–7000 B.C. Now they were faced with plants and animals familiar to modern Texans, and their projectile points had to be modified for the new kill. In 1983 the "Neanderthal Lady," the most intact human skeleton yet found from this period, was discovered near Austin, at a site known as the Wilson-Leonard site, which has also yielded hundreds of projectile points and tools from different occupations.

Baker Cave, near the Devil's River in Val Verde County, is another important site from this period, radiocarbon-dated at 7000 B.C. The arid climate of Southwest Texas and the protection provided by rock shelter at this campsite have preserved a remarkable array of plant and animal remains, yielding specific information on many aspects of ancient diet, including the extensive use of snakes as a dietary supplement.

By 6500 B.C., the old Paleo-Indian traditions began to wane, and regional cultures developed among the Native Americans of the Texas area. This new pattern, called the Archaic, is easily distinguished from the Paleo-Indian by the appearance of new kinds of projectile points, grinding tools for processing plant foods, and an emphasis on hunting white-tailed deer and other animals found in what were essentially modern-day environments.

☆ Thomas R. Hester, professor of anthropology at the University of Texas at San Antonio, gave this information on prehistoric Indians in Texas. Want to learn more about them? Get Professor Hester's book *Digging into South Texas Prehistory* (San Antonio: Corona, 1980) from your local bookstore or library.

Prehistoric Hunters and Gatherers

For more than ten thousand years people walked over the land of Texas hunting and gathering the food they needed to live. From the earliest human presence during the Ice Age until contact with Spaniards wiped out or changed their cultures, the Paleo-Indians and later Indians sagely used the fruits of the wild to sustain themselves. In East Texas, the Panhandle, and the El Paso area, Native Americans developed agricul-

Prehistoric hunters and gatherers in the Pecos River area created what anthropologists believe were religious symbols on rock surfaces. This 1937 watercolor by Forrest Kirkland precisely re-creates a Panther Cave mural in Val Verde County. Courtesy of the Texas Memorial Museum, Austin.

ture, but in central, southern, and southwest Texas, there was no agriculture until the Spanish introduced it in the eighteenth century.

As the glaciers receded from most of North America, the environment became more hospitable, allowing ancient Indian populations to grow and to spread throughout Texas. Hunters and gatherers, these people exploited wild plant foods and game animals in a systematic and efficient way. Although such a way of life is often labeled backward or savage, it is actually a very flexible and adaptable strategy for living. Far from having a hand-to-mouth, haphazard existence, a hunting and gathering culture relies on an intimate knowledge of its surroundings, the different habitats used by animals and plants, and a schedule for exploiting the animals and seasonally available plants, nuts, and berries.

Paleo-Indians lived from hunting and plant-food collecting, but their options for gathering were limited compared with the range of foods that began to appear as the climate warmed, after about 6000 B.C. As hunting and gathering became the dominant life-style, a culture developed that anthropologists and archaeologists call the Archaic.

White-tailed deer and an occasional bison were the favored prey of the early hunters and gatherers in central Texas, where small game was also plentiful. The Indians there also relied heavily on acorns for food, especially after oaks began to proliferate around 3500 B.C. The local people harvested, processed, and stored great quantities of acorns, which they used to make meal, mush, bread, and cakes. Heaps of fire-cracked rocks known as burned rock middens, found all across central Texas, probably were used in processing the acorns. In addition to their gathering, these Indians relied heavily on hunting. They made—and left behind at their campsites—large numbers of projectile points (arrowheads) and other stone tools chipped from the flint found abundantly in this area.

Two different life-styles developed among the hunters and gatherers in southern Texas, based on the different diets the environment offered. The Indians who lived along the coast could harvest shellfish, including oysters and conchs. They became so adept at this they left behind great piles of shells called shell middens. They even used the abundant shells for tools, a handy substitute for the flint found farther inland.

The southern Indians who did not border the sea followed patterns more like those to the north. South Texas was more lush than it is now; there were fewer mesquites and many more streams and springs. This landscape supported a thriving plant life, and the Indians there probably depended more heavily on the plant foods they gathered than on the deer, rabbits, and occasional bison they obtained through hunting. The women and children did most of the foraging for dietary mainstays, which included river mussels (clams) and land snails that were good sources of protein.

Out to the west and in the southwest part of Texas, hunting and gathering peoples camped in rock shelters and coves. The arid climate of the region has helped preserve many normally perishable plant, hide, and fiber artifacts that give marvelous clues to their daily life. In the lower Pecos region where the Pecos, Devil's, and Rio Grande rivers meet, archaeologists have been able to reconstruct the environment of the past nine thousand years and to study various facets of hunting and gathering and the impressive art these people practiced, such as the rock art of Panther Cave in Val Verde County. Although the region is rugged and forbidding, the ancient Indians developed ways to use effectively the food resources cached in the canyons and rivers.

The life-style the hunters and gatherers followed in Texas yielded them not only a relatively reliable and adequate diet, but also a social system that gave support and, judging from the little evidence available, the impetus and time for art. Indeed, a hunting and gathering life generally requires less effort and causes less stress than primitive farming—a fact that has led one anthropologist to describe theirs as the original leisure society.

☆ Materials on Texas' hunting and gathering peoples were submitted by Thomas R. Hester, professor of anthropology at the University of Texas at San Antonio. To help you begin exploring Texas' Indian history for yourself, you could get a copy of *A Field Guide to the Stone Artifacts of Texas* by E. S. Turner and T. R. Hester (Austin: Texas Monthly Press, 1985).

Prehistoric Farmers

The concept of saving seed, of not eating all the food available but instead holding some back that it might be grown again, revolutionized human life. Over the whole span of history and prehistory, less than one percent of human existence has been organized around this concept, farming. In Texas, the relatively settled way of life based at least partly on farming developed in the far west, the Panhandle, and the northwest in late prehistoric times.

Not many of these ancient settlements survived until the coming of the Europeans. Many were abandoned; others persisted, but with greatly reduced populations. Only in the northeast Texas woodlands did village life flourish; there some Caddoan-speaking tribes lived and farmed when the Spanish arrived. They had been there, these Caddos, for over a thousand years — since at least A.D. 800. They and their related groups had dominated an area that stretched from the middle of east Texas northward into the Ozarks.

Caddo life was very different from that of other Indians in Texas. Caddos were sedentary rather than migratory. They built more substantial houses, made more varied pottery, and even distinguished individuals of high status by the use of costume

items, such as beads of freshwater pearl. They were an industrious people, organized into a society that was more complex than that of their neighbors to the west.

Most Caddo tribes lived in small villages or hamlets located on easily farmed soils near streams or rivers. A typical settlement consisted of several pole-and-thatched houses; some houses were mud-plastered. At least by the time Europeans observed them, most dwellings were built large enough to house from two to eight nuclear families.

These households were the unit of both production and consumption; they were the centers around which everyday life was organized. Gardens provided beans, squash, sunflowers, and especially corn, which became the most common of the cultivated crops, although its relative importance varied from one Caddoan group to another. The diet was completed by a variety of wild foods, most important of which were the white-tailed deer and hardwood nuts, including hickories, walnuts, and acorns. These wild food resources provided dietary variety and helped prevent nutritional stresses that can result from high intakes of corn. Partial reliance on the foods nature supplied also acted as

Early Caddos in the Neches Valley, which would later be East Texas, had enough corn and wild foods to develop a vast trading network to obtain other supplies. Courtesy of Texas Parks and Wildlife Department.

a buffer against the loss of cultivated crops from drought, pest, and diseases.

Each village functioned independently in its daily affairs, but ties and positions of leadership united the individual communities into larger groups. Archaeological evidence, including regionally distinctive decorations on pottery vessels and the existence of ritual centers, indicates that larger groupings of Caddos existed even in prehistoric times. By the time the Span-iards came across them, the villagers living in the central portion of East Texas were organized into tribes, and the tribes into a confederacy, sometimes called the Kadohadacho, or "true Caddo."

Caddoan society was hierarchical. The Caddo confederacy of east Texas was organized with at least three ranks of officials. Even the prehistoric Caddos must have recognized some status differentiation, judging from the marked differences

11

in the amount of effort put into burying various individuals.

Caddoan society, especially in prehistoric times, was also apparently ritualistic. Ceremonial centers, the least frequent but most striking of the known prehistoric Caddoan sites, are distinguished by the presence of earthen mounds. Centers vary considerably in size and complexity, perhaps reflecting differences in the degree of sociopolitical integration among various Caddoan groups. The smaller centers appear primarily to have been special places for religious rituals. Their most distinctive feature is a mound, sometimes more than one, that contains a sequence of structures that have been destroyed, capped with earth, and then rebuilt on the earthen platform. These structures may have been temples.

The major centers are different, more complex. They served as seats of civic, economic, and religious power, as nodes in far-reaching interregional exchange systems, and as special mortuaries for elite members of the society. These diverse functions caused them to have more varied features and more kinds of artifacts than those found at either lesser centers or village sites. Only three major centers have been investigated in Texas; the best-known is Caddoan Mounds State Historic Site on the Neches River, near Alto. Though few in number, these centers have yielded the most extraordinary objects, including human-effigy smoking pipes sculptured in stone, copper-covered ear ornaments, engraved marine-shell pendants, elongated celts (axe heads), unusually long stone knives, and other items that were used in rituals or to signify high social status.

The apparent success of the Caddos over a thousand years of prehistory and history stemmed partly from their diverse economy, which included trading, and partly from the social and religious customs and institutions they developed, which integrated the separate villages into cohesive and apparently peaceful larger social groups. The coming of the Spaniards, who established their first mission in the area in 1690, interrupted all that. Today, only a few thousand Caddos live as a tribe, and that is in Indian Territory in Oklahoma — far from the land of their ancestors.

☆ This information on the Caddo Indians was supplied by Dee Ann Story, professor of anthropology at the University of Texas at Austin. To learn more about the Indian tribes of Texas, you could read W. W. Newcomb, Jr., *The Indians of Texas: From Prehistoric to Modern Times* (Austin: University of Texas Press, 1961).

The Spanish Search for Gold

Gold was not the only thing the early Spaniards sought in Texas, but perhaps it was not the least of what they hoped to gain. Alvar Núñez Cabeza de Vaca had

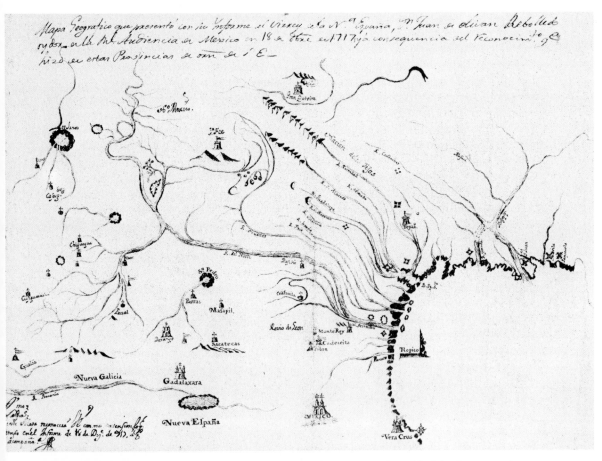

A 1717 map of New Spain indicates that the Wichita Indian community of Quivira (top center) near the Arkansas River was still used as a reference point by the Spanish long after Coronado's discovery that Quivira held no gold.

been to Texas, and he did not deny the persistent rumors that seven cities of gold awaited the gallant leader who would capture them.

Cabeza de Vaca had not intended to visit Texas. In 1528 he had been aboard one of five homemade boats that were the remnants of an ill-fated Spanish expedi-tion to "La Florida." When his boat was shipwrecked on the Texas coast at the "Isle of Malhado" (probably Galveston Island), he found himself in a part of New Spain that no Spanish eyes had ever seen before. Of the three hundred men who survived the original wreck off Florida, only Cabeza and three others would ever re-

13

turn to what is now Mexico. The journey these four made, beset by sickness and hostile coastal Indians, was the first recorded European intrusion into the interior of Texas. The four—Cabeza, Andrés Dorantes de Carranza, Alonso del Castillo Maldonado, and Dorantes's black slave Estebanico—lived among Texas Indians for eight years. They came to be regarded as healers and medicine men and thus were able to travel from tribe to tribe until they eventually reached Spanish settlements.

Intrigued by the rumors of seven cities of gold in the interior that Cabeza de Vaca reported after his rescue, New Spain's viceroy, Antonio de Mendoza, purchased Estebanico from Dorantes and sent him as a guide for Marcos de Niza, a friar who was to make a preliminary search for the seven cities. Estebanico was killed by Pueblo Indians, but Friar Marcos returned to Mexico convinced that the legendary riches existed.

To find and claim his anticipated wealth, Mendoza appointed Francisco Vásquez de Coronado, governor of New Galacia, to lead an expedition north into the unknown country. Coronado gathered an army of a thousand men at the small Mexican town of Compostela, where they were reviewed by the viceroy in February, 1540. Then, traveling with fifteen hundred horses and mules, the largest European expedition ever to penetrate the present United States, they marched north, conquering pueblo after pueblo.

While they were at Pecos Pueblo in present New Mexico an Indian they named "The Turk" convinced Coronado and his men that the wealth they sought lay to the east in a fabulous land called Quivira. Off they set, venturing onto the Texas plains in search of gold. Full of optimism, they offered a Mass of thanksgiving in the Palo Duro Canyon, near Amarillo.

Their optimism would give way to disappointment, though. Entering present-day Kansas, they at last found the long-sought Quivira. Instead of seven cities, it proved to be only a modest Wichita Indian village. Instead of gold, it held the staples of Indians' daily life. Disheartened and weary, the expedition turned back south. Before returning to Mexico, though, they tortured and executed "The Turk" for his trickery. It was not until many years had passed that members of the expedition reminiscing about their travels recognized that the land they had explored could itself have been the wealth they had sought in vain.

The search for El Dorado (the gold) did not end, however, with Coronado's negative report. Other explorers seeking gold as well as fame traversed the unmapped lands of Texas. In 1541 Hernando de Soto entered Texas from the east in search of gold. That summer he died somewhere in eastern Texas, his dream of wealth unfulfilled. In 1601, partly to lay to rest once and for all the reports of gold and partly to establish a colony, Juan de Oñate led an *entrada* into Texas. The runaway livestock from his short-lived settlement may have contributed to a future source of wealth in Texas: the longhorn cattle.

Deep in the New World, the desire to conquer, to gain wealth and power, had taken root. Indeed, according to historian Roberto Mario Salmón, this search for "the

14

fabulous" spawned a rich folkloric and historic tradition among Spanish Mexicans.

Later expeditions would seek forms of wealth and power that would prove less elusive than the gold—land and cattle. But together, these quests would eventually map the Texas frontier and open the land for the permanent settlements that followed.

☆ These facts about Spanish efforts to find Quivira and gold were supplied by William C. Griggs, executive director and president of the Harris County Heritage Society. You can learn more about the various facets of Spanish exploration in what is now Texas by reading a classic treatment: Herbert E. Bolton, *Spanish Exploration in the Southwest, 1542–1706.*

The Missions

The cross and the sword came together to Texas. What the Spanish crown wanted to conquer for its possible wealth and as a buffer zone against hostile Indians and aggressive French explorers, the Spanish church desired to claim for its Lord. Together, they devised something new in the North American colonial experience: the mission.

In the late 1680s, Alonzo de León, governor of Coahuila, got word of a French presence in Texas, the outpost founded by René Robert Cavalier, Sieur de la Salle, a short distance inland from Matagorda Bay. Alarmed, he launched eleven expeditions to locate the trespassers. Even when he found their fort in ruins following a successful attack by Karankawa Indians, he did not rest. He wanted to establish a tangible claim in Texas, a signpost to the French or others that the land belonged to Spain.

In 1690 De León accompanied Father Damien Massanet northeastward to the Trinity River, where they established the mission San Francisco de los Tejas to work among the Caddo Indians. A second mission, Santísimo Nombre de María, was established on the Neches River. The Indians were at first curious about the priests and their rituals, but within three years most had drifted away from the mission. Because the mission was located so far from a source of food, the priests were forced to rely on the Indians, who grew to resent efforts by the soldiers stationed there to make them labor for the mission. Within a few years the mission was withdrawn, having succeeded only in serving notice that the Spanish intended to retain control of East Texas.

Early in the eighteenth century the Spanish launched a new wave of missionary activity in East Texas to convert the Indians to the Spanish religion and life-style. The friars established missions, while nearby the soldiers set up forts, or presidios, to protect them.

From the beginning the Spanish viewed the missions not only as religious outposts

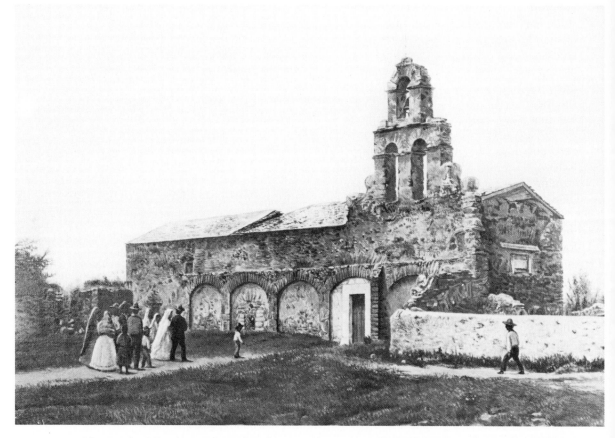

Obeying the Spanish viceroy's orders that East Texas missions be withdrawn south to safety near San Antonio de Béxar, San Juan Capistrano mission relocated in 1731. Theodore Gentilz portrayed a wedding party enroute to the mission chapel more than a century later. Courtesy of the Daughters of the Republic of Texas Library, San Antonio.

but also as an agency for frontier control. Although friars from Mexico administered them, the Spanish government paid for them and reinforced them with presidios. The missionaries seem to have shared the state's interest in introducing Spanish ways to the Indians, though perhaps their motives were different. Both wanted the In-

dians to abandon their nomadic life-style and settle permanently in or near the missions. The Franciscan friars were taught native dialects so that they could communicate the faith, but they were instructed gradually to shift into Spanish, weaning the Indians from their mother tongues.

Missionaries also trained their converts

in European crafts and arts. They taught stone masonry, carpentry, farming, animal husbandry, weaving, leather tanning, and blacksmithing. The arts they offered included both the secular and the sacred and ranged from church music and choral singing to dancing and painting. The idea was that once steeped in Spanish culture, the Indians would be not only good converts but also good subjects of the crown. Indeed, the missions were intended to be training centers to acquaint them with the municipal responsibilities of Spanish subjects. The mission plaza would introduce the converts to its secular parallel, the town plaza.

The missionary system was designed to be temporary. Once the Indians were converted to Christianity and the Spanish way of life, the missions were to be secularized. That is, while the church would remain the spiritual center of the community, the rest of the mission's property would be distributed to the nearby landowners. Originally, the Spanish thought this would take about one generation; in fact, conversion often went much slower, secularization somewhat faster. In 1793 Mission San Antonio de Valero became the first mission to be fully secularized. The era of church and state cooperation in the mission venture was drawing to a close. The legacy was mixed.

Most Texas Indians resisted the new religion and customs, leaving the missions after a few years. Where only the sword (the presidio) had reinforced the friars' efforts, as in East Texas, the missions' effectiveness had depended on the soldiers' presence; when the presidios were removed, the missions declined. Most were shut down and their friars moved to San Antonio. There, in San Antonio, a colony of descendants of Spanish settlers in the Canary Islands was established in 1731. This civil settlement was what was needed to bring stability to the efforts of the mission and the presidio. Together, these three communities gave birth to a successful settlement that endures to this day.

☆ Background on the Spanish mission system was furnished by Felix D. Almaráz, Jr., professor of history at the University of Texas at San Antonio. A good book on the missions in the San Antonio area is Marion A. Habig's *The Alamo Chain of Missions: A History of San Antonio's Five Old Missions* (Chicago: Franciscan Herald Press, 1968).

The Austin Colony

Spain had never welcomed foreigners in any Spanish territories, rarely even allowed them there. Foreign settlement in Texas was forbidden, with few exceptions, for close to three hundred years. But in Texas the year 1820 found Spain desperate for new ways to battle the Comanches, who regularly raided San Antonio and made life there nearly impossible. Rugged farmers could help exterminate the Comanches,

Though Stephen F. Austin was known as a skillful negotiator, Henry McArdle's 1885 painting portrayed him reaching for his rifle in response to a colonist's warning of an Indian attack. Courtesy of the Texas State Capitol, Austin.

reasoned the government, and at the same time develop the local agriculture, especially cotton, adding to the crown's coffers.

The year 1820 found others desperate, too. In the Mississippi River Valley a bank panic of the year before had devastated all too many people. Even small farmers had lost their land, when creditors demanded immediate payment. Anglo farmers were looking west for a place to start anew. A few adventurous families had already moved into eastern Texas and, lacking a means of securing legal titles, had squatted on the land.

The stage was set; need answered need when in December of 1820 Moses Austin secured an empresario contract from the authorities in San Antonio. The land grant allowed him to settle in Texas three hundred of the "right sort" of North Americans —Roman Catholics, all former residents of Spanish Louisiana (which included present Missouri), who agreed to pledge their loyalty to Spain.

Moses Austin was near desperation himself. The Saint Louis bank for which he was principal stockholder had collapsed in 1819, as speculative values were falling and the first U.S. depression took hold. Austin had held a Spanish passport since 1796, when he had moved from Virginia to Missouri during a brief relaxation of the rules against foreign settlement. There he had prospered in lead mining, banking, and the mercantile business, and he had remained in Missouri after the transfer of the territory from Spanish to French to American authority following the Louisiana Purchase in 1803. Perhaps remembering his earlier prosperity under

Spanish authority, Austin saw the colonizing of Texas as a way to recoup his losses. Details of the grant he secured remained vague when he returned home early in 1821, but he had no trouble lining up farmers in the Mississippi Valley who wanted to move to Texas under his auspices. The sixty-year-old Austin was not to realize his dream of colonizing the Spanish lands. He died in June, weakened by the rigors of his return trip through the wilderness from Missouri to Texas.

He left the charge to recover the family fortunes to his twenty-seven-year-old son, Stephen Fuller Austin. The young Austin was a diplomat and a visionary. He set out at once for San Antonio, where the governor recognized him as heir to the contract. Austin chose land along either side of the Colorado and Brazos rivers near the coast for his grant, then returned to Missouri to sign up colonists. There was no shortage of applicants for his land titles, which sold for only a fraction of the cost of U.S. land.

When he returned with colonists at the close of 1821, Austin learned that Mexico had won independence from Spain, which meant that he had to travel to Mexico City to reconfirm the contract with the new government. That accomplished, he returned to Texas in August, 1823, and found a number of settlers awaiting titles. It was almost a year, though, before deeds were issued by the state-appointed land commissioner, Philip Nering de Bogel, Baron de Bastrop.

By 1824 Mexican liberals had gained control of the new government, and Austin's plan to charge each settler twelve and one-half cents per acre for 640 acres had to be abandoned. Instead, each head of family, widows as well as males, received a league (4,428 acres) of pasture land and a *labor* (177 acres) of irrigable farmland for a modest payment of sixty dollars in fees to the land commissioner, the surveyor, and the clerk making the deeds. The empresario received no cash; instead he was awarded five leagues and five *labores* for each 100 families settled. Austin's contract for 300 families, later known as the Old Three Hundred, entitled him to 69,075 acres if he got them all settled within six years.

Austin was disappointed by the cancellation of the fee system he had counted on to restore the family fortunes, but he pushed ahead, settling 272 families under his first contract. He quickly found that the premium land awarded to him as empresario was difficult to sell when every immigrant family could secure 4,605 acres as a headright. Settlers from the United States flocked to the colony for the bargain in land. From those without cash, Austin accepted a cow and a calf per ten dollars owed, a standard valuation then, and he also extended credit. An even more popular arrangement was "going halves," meaning that a man of wealth, such as Austin, his brother, or his associate Samuel May Williams, would pay the fees in exchange for half of the headright.

Austin ultimately received three additional contracts, allowing the settlement of 900 more families: land between the Brazos and Colorado watersheds below the Old Spanish Road from San Antonio to Nacogdoches, a small area above the road in present Travis County, and an extension of the coastal area eastward to the San Jacinto River. By 1831, Austin claimed 5,655 residents in his colonies; he had earned well over 200,000 acres of premium land along the lower Brazos and elsewhere. Other empresarios, both native Mexican and Anglo, had less success than Austin.

Austin's "capital," established at San Felipe, became the center for Anglo-Texan activities. Until 1828 Austin acted as judge, mayor, and "father confessor" for the colony, but in 1828 an *ayuntamiento,* or council that generally combined the functions of city and county governments, assumed the burden of governing. Incoming settlers brought U.S. political and judicial traditions, which they followed, largely disregarding Mexican laws. Because Mexico was a republic, Anglo-Texans wrongly assumed that they enjoyed the same privileges as they had had in the United States, and the differences between English common law and Roman (Spanish/Mexican) law caused a great deal of misunderstanding and conflict. Colonists had no guarantees of freedom of speech or press, the right to assemble, or the right to trial by jury, bail, or formal indictment. The requirement to be Roman Catholic was clear indication that there was—in theory, at least—no religious freedom. In practice, the requirement was rarely enforced; settlers had to declare themselves Catholics to receive their land, but no priest was sent to the colonies until 1831, and he stayed only a year and was of a liberal persuasion.

Roman law as Spain and then Mexico developed it had certain advantages that the Anglos quickly recognized, such as a homestead provision that exempted a man's house and the tools of his trade from seizure by creditors and a community property law that excluded property in the wife's name from seizure for debt. These provisions were adopted by the Texas Republic and remained in Texas law into modern times.

Mexico also had no land tax or income tax, depending instead on customs duties to pay the cost of government. Austin's colony enjoyed a six-year exemption from paying tariff. That this was a temporary provision was misunderstood by Anglo-Texans, and resentment ran high in 1830, when collection of the standard Mexican duties began in Texas ports.

For the most part, most Anglos in Texas followed Austin's lead in becoming good citizens of their adopted country. But just as Spanish authorities had anticipated, Texas settlements faced a profound clash of cultures. After 1830 tensions between the Texans and the central government mounted, and by 1835 they had escalated to the breaking point.

☆ Margaret Swett Henson, adjunct assistant professor of history at the University of Houston–Clear Lake, provided the information on Austin's Colony. To learn more about the colony's founder, you could read Eugene C. Barker's *The Life of Stephen F. Austin, Founder of Texas, 1793–1836*, first published in 1926 and reissued by the University of Texas Press, Austin, in 1969.

A Mexican Texas

The rivalries of Europe have more than once determined the fate of the Americas. When Napoleon toppled the royal government of Spain in 1808, he sounded the death knell of the Spanish empire. Spain's colonies in America were left to drift unattended, and local insurgents, recognizing the empire's vulnerability, began to challenge Spanish rule.

One of the most celebrated early challenges came in 1810, when, amid social and political unrest created by the Napoleonic invasion of Iberia, Father Miguel Hidalgo issued his "Grito de Dolores" (Cry of Anguish), a list of grievances against Spain. Father Hidalgo and his followers declared

themselves loyal to the Spanish monarchy but asserted that local people could govern New Spain, or Mexico, better than the administrators sent to them by Napoleon's puppet king, even if they were Spanish.

Hidalgo's movement failed and he himself was executed, but by 1811 the repercussions of his revolution reached Texas. There proponents of Mexican independence collided with defenders of royalism on several battlefields. In 1812 a filibustering expedition led by a veteran of Hidalgo's campaign, Bernardo Gutiérrez de Lara, and an American ally, Augustus Magee, invaded Texas from the east. Magee's rag-tag army captured Nacogdoches in August, 1812, and the following April they proclaimed Texas free of Spain. Subsequently they defeated a Spanish military unit at La Bahía and captured San Antonio before being defeated by General Joaquín de Arredondo in an action at the Medina River. In 1819 Dr. James Long invaded Texas, also declaring it independent. He, too, was defeated. Then, on July 19, 1821, the governor of Texas led the community in proclaiming Mexico independent two months before the triumph of revolutionaries in Mexico City.

The change from Spanish control to Mexican direction of affairs meant more in style than in substance. The traditional institutions—the church, the army, the governmental hierarchy, and the landed aristocracy—continued to control daily affairs. Mexican nationalism was a new experience for most, particularly for the Tejanos, whose loyalty to the region where they lived exceeded their loyalty to their new central government. Even at the height of Spanish imperialism, the great distance from Mexico City worked against integration of the region into the central government. The turmoil of revolution and the uncertainty about the final nature of the Mexican state magnified the effects of that distance.

Because of the many problems of the Mexican government, the frontier provinces —or states, as they would soon be called in emulation of the political arrangement in the United States—continued to feel only the shadow of the traditional centralized authority, not its full force. Regional autonomy and local control gained ground because of the absence of central enforce-

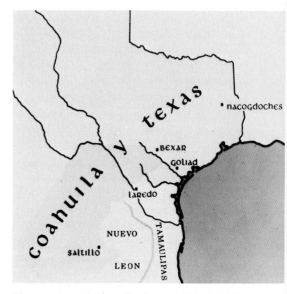

The creation of the unified state of Coahuila y Texas alarmed both Tejano and Anglo inhabitants of Texas in the 1820s and 1830s. With the seat of government far south in Saltillo, Texans feared that their interests would be shunted aside. Courtesy of the University of Texas Institute of Texan Cultures, San Antonio.

ment. Following the short-lived empire of Agustín Iturbide, Mexican nationalists inaugurated a federal form of government under the Constitution of 1824. This document established as pure a state's-rights government as ever existed, an arrangement that was completely alien to three hundred years of tradition for everyone in New Spain. The Tejanos, and later the Anglo-Americans in Texas, liked the fact that most political affairs were shifted to state direction but chafed when Texas was combined with Coahuila, shifting the focus of their regional government from San Antonio to Saltillo.

During the first decade of Mexican independence, the federalists and centralists competed for the power to direct the nation. In Texas this affected the important question of legal immigration from the United States. The Iturbide government agreed to honor the Spanish government's decision, made just as it had passed from authority, to permit Moses Austin to introduce American colonists into Texas. The new federal government turned such matters over to the state governments, with some restrictions, and in turn the government of Coahuila y Texas continued, indeed encouraged for a time, the legal settlement of Americans and others in Texas. The liberality of the colonization laws of the 1820s was accepted with gratitude by the first generation of colonists. Later, when centralists regained control and began to tighten immigration policies, the Texas colonists rebelled against them.

The presidency of Guadalupe Victoria (1824–28) under the federal constitution had virtually no effect on Texas, which looked to Saltillo for most government direction. But the succeeding administrations of Vicente Guerrero, Anastacio Bustamante, and Antonio López de Santa Anna produced an escalating alarm in Texas. Guerrero abolished slavery, which many Texans regarded as crucial to their way of life; Bustamante's administration promulgated the Law of April 6, 1830, which cut off all Anglo immigration; and Santa Anna abrogated the federalist constitution and proclaimed all power once again in central, that is, his own, hands. Relations rapidly deteriorated between Tejanos and Texans on the periphery of Mexico and their central government.

If San Antonio de Béxar had retained the mantle of regional leadership, perhaps the tensions of 1835 and 1836 would have been resolved by peaceful means. But as events demonstrated, decisions made by national leaders in Mexico City were resented. As had Spain, Mexico addressed problems in Texas only in times of crisis. Unlike Spain, which by keeping its hold over Texas loose managed to retain it for more than a century, Mexico under Santa Anna moved to tighten its control and ultimately lost Texas entirely.

⭐ Felix D. Almaráz, Jr., professor of history at the University of Texas at San Antonio, provided this information on Mexican Texas. He has written a biography of a Spanish governor of Texas that can give you more insight into the period, as well as the individual. It is *Tragic Cavalier: Governor Manuel Salcedo of Texas, 1809–1813* (Austin: University of Texas Press, 1971).

Life of a Colonist

It was not so much a new way of life that Anglo settlers sought in Texas as a new, debt-free start on the old ways. It is not surprising, then, that life in Austin's colo-

A traveler from the United States who visited this planter's estate near Brazoria, Texas, in 1831, wrote that his host had provided an excellent meal, which "consisted chiefly of venison and a fine turkey, and was accompanied with excellent coffee." Many American settlers in nineteenth-century Texas built dogtrot homes like this (two rooms with a passageway between and a single roof). Illustration from A Visit to Texas *(New York: Goodrich & Wiley, 1834).*

nies after 1824 resembled that in the United States. Colonists who had been townfolk before gathered near San Felipe, Brazoria, or Harrisburg and were townfolk again, re-creating the villages they had known back home. Frontier families that had wanted elbow room in Kentucky were no more interested in seeing the smoke from their neighbors' chimneys in Texas; they shunned the towns and chose isolated homesteads just as they had done before.

Similarities in life-styles were reinforced by increasing commerce between Anglo colonies in Texas and the states. By the late 1820s sailing vessels regularly visited Texas from New Orleans, bringing needed supplies to the Brazos River communities and Galveston Bay and exchanging them for agricultural and forest products. Money was more scarce in Texas than it had been in the United States. Settlers depended on an international currency, gold and silver coins from around the world, but there were never enough of them, and a barter economy soon evolved. Certain items had a standard value, for example a cow and a calf equaled ten dollars.

While some frontier families preferred to continue to live in rude log cabins — and others had no choice in the matter — villagers and the more affluent class quickly chose to board over the logs once sawmills were established on the Brazos River and Buffalo Bayou in the late 1820s. Glass windows, paint, and nicely finished interiors became more common by 1830.

Tree stumps were left to rot in some village streets, leading some visitors to assume incorrectly that there was no plan of development. In reality, though, each village was laid out in an orderly fashion with streets running along cardinal compass points as Mexican law required. In San Felipe each block was divided into six regular lots, 120 feet by 180 feet, and ten-acre garden plots on the outskirts of town were available to the elite, who might want more privacy and relief from the noise and filth of the town square.

Village stores carried imported staples such as flour, sugar, pickled meat, tea, coffee, kitchen ware, farming tools, medicine, and sewing materials. In addition, merchants offered local items such as eggs, butter, fruits, nuts, and corn that had been brought in for barter. A butcher at San Felipe in 1828 offered portions of beef at four cents per pound. Special orders placed with local merchants for goods from New Orleans usually arrived in a month or less, depending on when vessels sailed for the Crescent City, a three- to four-day voyage from the mouth of the Brazos River if wind and tides were favorable.

Villages offered some professional services, too. Lawyers were everywhere, although many were the "cornstalk" variety, meaning that they lacked training or licenses or both. At least three doctors practiced medicine in San Felipe, and they, like the physicians in the other villages, made house calls to treat both white families and slaves in the village and on nearby plantations. Schools were irregular, meeting whenever a teacher was available; terms were usually short, but most boys and girls did attend some elementary-level classes. One San Felipe merchant maintained a lending library stocked with books by such popular writers of the day as Sir Walter Scott. Only churches were lacking. The Roman Catholic church was supported by the state, but the only resident priest sent to the Anglo colonies was Father Michael Muldoon, and he stayed only from 1831 until 1832. Itinerant Protestant missionaries — Baptists, Methodists, and an occasional Presbyterian — sometimes visited and conducted surreptitious services. After 1834 moderate freedom of religion was allowed.

Visiting, barbecues, and dances constituted the standard fare for entertainment in colonial Texas. The major U.S. celebrations, such as the Fourth of July, were observed, and at least once, in March, 1826, a special gala was held in San Felipe in honor of the adoption of the Mexican constitution. Merchants provided a feast, and Brown Austin, the empresario's brother, fired twenty-three salvos from the town's cannon in honor of the states and territories of the Mexican Republic, while a red, white, and green national flag floated overhead. A visiting circus and fireworks display from New Orleans attracted a large crowd in San Felipe on another occasion.

Contrary to the popular myth, Texas was no harder on women than Kentucky had been on their mothers. Their role and their work were much the same in Texas as in the United States. Drudgery prevailed for those without slave help in the house and the kitchen garden. Frontier women spun their own thread and wove their own cloth to fashion their families' garments, and sometimes they made clothing from buckskin. Women in the villages bought cloth and occasionally ordered ready-made wearing apparel from New Orleans. Several women in San Felipe were part-time dressmakers, and a few supplemented the family income by selling surplus foodstuffs or taking in roomers or boarders. A well-off family without slaves might employ a laundress from the lower classes, including native Mexican women. A number of women rode horseback for pleasure and for visiting, presumably using sidesaddles, and frontier women knew how to use a gun if they needed to. Rural women milked cows, fed hogs and chickens, tended turkeys and geese, and

planted the vegetable gardens. Contrary to some travel accounts, most Texans had a variety of foods in season. Critical visitors who complained about having only coffee, cornbread, and pork must have stopped only at destitute houses or houses where the weather, insects, or many visitors had demolished the food stores.

In fact, the similarities of life in the colonies with that the Americans had left behind must have given Mexican officials pause. With a "little America" growing up among them they must have feared what their Spanish predecessors had foreseen: the eventual movement to rejoin the colonies to their roots. With U.S. influence so strong, Mexican Texas would be, not a melting pot, but a boiling pot.

☆ This information was provided by Margaret Swett Henson, adjunct assistant professor of history at the University of Houston–Clear Lake. A classic early account of colonial life, although not without some factual errors, is Noah Smithwick's *The Evolution of a State: Or, Recollections of Old Texas Days,* first published in 1900, and re-issued, with illustrations by Charles Shaw, by the University of Texas Press in 1983.

Moving toward Revolution

Almost from the first the relationship between the Anglos and Mexicans in Texas was troubled, despite the efforts of people of good will on both sides. The Anglos' attitude of superiority did not sit well with the host nation, and the Anglos did not understand the Latin political concept of subjectship instead of citizenship. Still, most early immigrants who arrived during the mid-1820s, especially those who came to the grants of Stephen F. Austin, made genuine efforts to adjust to the new culture. Those who came to the Haden Edwards grant in East Texas, on the other hand, quarreled with authorities from the first, and the resulting Fredonian Rebellion in 1825–27 alarmed Mexican authorities, heightening fears of a possible Anglo takeover of their lands, a prospect that had troubled them since the days of Augustus Magee and James Long. Mexicans also worried about the intentions of the U.S. government after its minister, Joel Poinsett, offered to purchase lands west of the Sabine River. Thereafter they perceived almost every Anglo activity in Texas as some kind of "yankee plot" to take Texas from them and add it to the United States.

Mexican nationalists Lucas Alamán, Manuel de Mier y Terán, and José María Tornel in 1829 persuaded President Vicente Guerrero to abolish slavery in Mexico as one way to weaken the Texans. They also secured the passage of the Law of April 6, 1830, which stopped Anglo immigration, rerouted trade from the United States destined for Texas, instituted customs collections, placed the granting of land once more in the hands of the central government, and provided for sending convicts to Texas from Mexico as settlers. These measures provoked resentment among the Anglo population.

The first clash occurred at Anahuac, where the commander of the Mexican garrison, Juan Davis Bradburn, had angered the Anglos by beginning the collection of customs. He also required shipowners to obtain clearance papers from him, and he stopped granting land even to settlers already in Texas before the passage of the law. In 1832 Bradburn arrested several protestors, including William B. Travis and Patrick Jack, for their defiance, and angry Americans arrived to secure their release.

The Anglos drafted the Turtle Bayou Resolutions, a pledge of their loyalty to the Mexican Constitution of 1824 and their defiance of the central government, which they charged was ignoring the constitution. Anticipating violence, they sent John Austin to Velasco for a cannon. Colonel José de las Piedras arrived from Nacogdoches before bloodshed began, however, and he ordered the release of Travis and Jack. After relieving Bradburn of command, he returned to Nacogdoches, where he tried to prevent a similar occurrence by ordering the surrender of all firearms. The Texans did bring their guns to town, but once there, they used them against Piedras. And at Velasco, where he had arrived with the cannon intended for Anahuac, John Austin encountered the encampment of Colonel Domingo de Ugartechea. After a skirmish in which ten Anglos and five Mexicans died, Ugartechea surrendered. These three events, dubbed the "disturbances of 1832," marked the beginning of Anglo resistance to Mexico's centralist government.

The Anglos held a convention in September at San Felipe to pledge once more their loyalty and to request the reopening of land grants, exemption from taxes, and separate statehood within Mexico. The political chief at San Antonio promptly rejected their petition, so in January, 1833,

Soberano Congreso Gen.l de la Federasion Mexicana.

Los habitantes de Texas en convencion p.r medio de sus representantes electos y reunidos, con el mas alto respeto, suplican á la Soberania Nacional Mexicana: Que la Union que se establecio entre Coahuila y Texas, por la cual se incorporaron las dos Provincias antiguas en un Estado libre é independiente, bajo el nombre de "Estado de Coahuila y Texas", se disuelva, abrogue y cese perpetuamente: Y que los habitantes de Texas sean autorizados para establecer separadamente un Govierno de Estado, q.e sea acorde con la Constitucion Federal y Acta Constitutiva: Y q.e el Estado asi constituido, sea recivido é incorporado en la grande Confederacion Mexicana, y nivelado con los demas Estados de la Union. Para apoyar la base de esta solicitud, los q.e representan suplican, respetuosamente, al Soberano Congreso G.l fixe su atencion en las siguientes consideraciones.

El Decreto del Soberano Congreso G.l Constituyente, de f.ha 7 de Mayo de 1824, presupone una separacion entre Coahuila y Texas y garantiza á esta el derecho de tener un Govierno de Estado separado, en todo tiempo q.e se halle en condicion de pedirlo. Este Decreto ha previsto q.e "tan luego que Texas estuviera en aptitud de figurar como un Estado por si sola, lo participaria al Soberano Congreso G.l para su resolucion." El texto literal de esta clausula es claro é imperativo, y concede á Texas un derecho tan perfecto cual se pueda imaginar, solo q.e se presuma q.e el Soberano Congreso Constituyente, compuesto de los venerables Padres de la Republica, intentó entretener al buen pueblo de Texas p.r medio de una promesa ilusoria vistiendola con todo el aparato de un acto ó decreto legislativo. Los q.e representan tienen una veneracion mui profunda á ese Soberano Cuerpo, p.r lo q.e no pueden concevir la idea de q.e tal aplicacion se le ha de dar á sus actos, por sus sucesores patrioticos, el pre-

they met again, drafted the same resolutions, and asked Stephen F. Austin to carry their cause directly to Mexico City. He arrived while the harried acting president, Valentín Gómez Farías, was preoccupied with attempting to reform the army, the church, and the patterns of land ownership. A heated argument between the two men led Austin to write an inflammatory letter to San Antonio's *ayuntamiento* or governing council, urging Texas to declare its separate status. This letter quite naturally led to his arrest; he was detained for eighteen months.

Stunned Texans were quiet while Austin was in prison but grew more angry as time passed. When Austin finally was released in the summer of 1835, many anticipated his return and were ready to carry their feelings of resentment into active resistance.

☆ This material came from Archie P. McDonald, professor of history at Stephen F. Austin State University. For a reassessment of the events at Anahuac, read Margaret Swett Henson's book *Juan Davis Bradburn: A Reappraisal of the Mexican Commander of Anahuac* (College Station: Texas A&M University Press, 1982).

"Come and Take It"

When Stephen F. Austin returned to Texas in September, 1835, after an eighteen-month imprisonment, the issue of war or peace hung in the balance. A hush that had fallen over Texas after his arrest—a hush born of fear for Austin's safety—began to give way as incidents between local leaders and central authorities proliferated.

Not all unrest was confined to Texas; the Mexican nation was in the throes of conflict between centralists and states' righters. The military suppression of an at-

◀ *Stephen F. Austin delivered the Texans' proposal for separate Mexican statehood (first page shown here) to authorities in Mexico City in 1833. The Mexican government rejected their request, contributing further to the Texans' dissatisfaction. Courtesy of the Texas State Archives, Austin.*

tempt by the governor and legislature of Coahuila y Texas to move the state capital from Saltillo to Monclova alarmed Texans. For pragmatic as well as ideological reasons, the Texans were on the side of the states' righters and saw this use of force by the central government as fueling their resentments.

Then trouble flared again in Anahuac, when President Antonio López de Santa Anna sent a detachment under Antonio Tenorio there to enforce the custom law and collect tariffs. William B. Travis, who had been instigator of an earlier confrontation in Anahuac, had moved to San Felipe de Austin, but other disgruntled Anglos had risen to take his place in the resistance. Merchant Andrew Briscoe and DeWitt C. Harris were arrested for refusing to allow guards to inspect the contents of a box filled with rocks intended as ballast for a ship. Suspecting this was only a ruse to mask smuggling, the guards insisted on a search and, becoming alarmed, fired their weapons.

In June an ad hoc meeting at San Felipe sent Travis back to Anahuac to drive Tenorio away. Travis led about twenty-five men on the mission. When they arrived by barge via Galveston Bay, Tenorio's soldiers disappeared into the nearby woods, but Tenorio surrendered later that evening. The Mexican prisoners were sent to Brazorio, where they arrived in time for a Fourth of July party. There Travis's men were ridiculed and the Mexicans were treated as honored guests by Peace party advocates, who feared that this latest action would bring reprisals from the Mexican government. They were correct. General Martín Perfecto de Cós prepared to move his headquarters to San Antonio and demanded the surrender for military trial of "Juliano" Travis and the other "outlaws" who had captured Tenorio. This was too much for even the Peace party advocates.

Then Austin returned to Texas, and at a gathering at San Felipe on September 19, he declared: "War is our only recourse. There is no other remedy. We must defend our rights ourselves and our country by force of arms." Committees of safety called for a "Consultation," a sort of convention of all Texans to determine a course of action, but before it could meet the Mexican army made the decision for them.

Colonel Domingo de Ugartechea sent a patrol from San Antonio to Gonzales to confiscate a six-pound cannon used for

Artist Waldene Tausch's frieze on this monument near Gonzales pays homage to a small group of farmers and townspeople who resisted Mexican soldiers' attempts to confiscate a cannon in October, 1835, an early incident in the Texas Revolution. Courtesy of the Gonzales Inquirer.

defense against Indians. Alcalde (mayor) Andrew Ponton refused to release the cannon without written orders. While the patrol returned for the orders, he buried the cannon. As the word of its attempted confiscation spread, men arrived to defend the cannon. They dug it up, readied it for battle, and prepared a flag with a drawing of a cannon and the words "COME AND TAKE IT." Their elected leader, Colonel J. H. Moore, defied Lieutenant Francisco Castañeda's one hundred troops to take the cannon, and the Mexicans returned to San

Antonio because they had not been instructed to use force.

More Texans arrived, including Stephen F. Austin, whom they elected as their chief. He agreed to lead them to San Antonio, where they laid siege to Cós's installation. Meanwhile, at the Consultation, Texans established an interim government, provided for an army, and sent Austin, Branch T. Archer, and William Wharton to the United States to seek private or public assistance. Edward Burleson succeeded Austin at San Antonio. In early December Burleson prepared to withdraw from the city, but Ben Milam challenged the group instead to follow him into the city in battle. The day rang with the rallying cry "Who will go into San Antonio with old Ben Milam?" More than three hundred did so,

and after a five-day battle (December 5–9, 1835), the Texans defeated Cós and ordered him to return to Mexico.

Gonzales has been called the "Lexington of the Texas Revolution," but it was the loss not of a cannon but of San Antonio that brought the larger armies of Santa Anna north to the major battles of that revolution.

☆ This account of the confrontation at Gonzales comes from Archie P. McDonald, professor of history at Stephen F. Austin State University. For an idea of the Mexicans' view of the events of the Texas revolution, read the excerpts from memoirs and diaries of the Mexican officers in Carlos E. Castaneda's *The Mexican Side of the Texas Revolution* (Salem, N.H.: Ayer, 1976).

The Alamo

Perhaps they breathed easy—those Texans caught up in the escalating events that would bring a revolution. As they entered the winter of 1835–36 with their army holding the two strongest presidios in Texas, La Bahía (Goliad) and the Alamo at San Antonio, perhaps they felt secure and even optimistic. Or perhaps they nursed secret fears about a developing leadership crisis and dangerous vulnerability if the government to the south turned its full attention on the upstart Anglos.

Sam Houston commanded the Texas forces; he commanded, but he hardly controlled. The Consultation that had placed him in command ignored his advice from the start and, against Houston's better judgment, commissioned a small force to head south to Matamoros to regain confiscated lands. At San Antonio and Goliad, only volunteers stood guard, and at the Alamo, following their successful assault on the Mexicans, the Texans lacked direction. Stephen F. Austin had been dispatched to the United States to seek aid. His successor, Edward Burleson, had left before the charge on the city; Ben Milam had been killed in the battle.

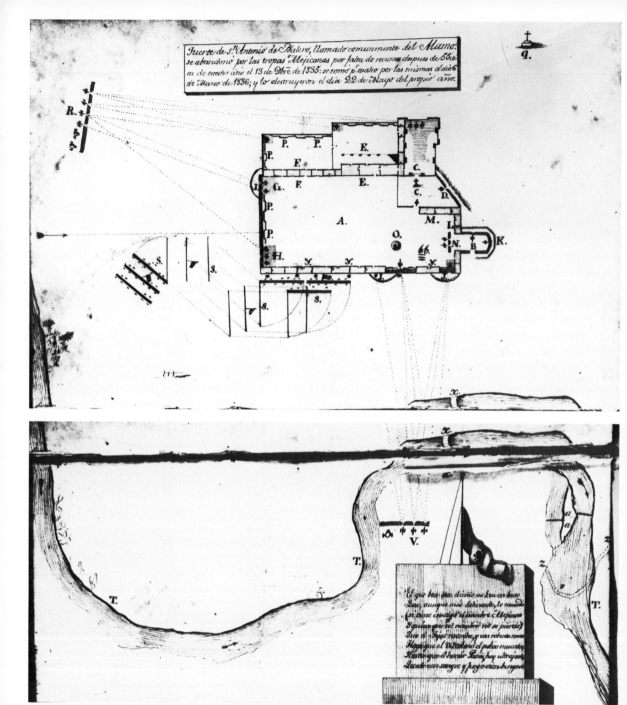

In an official military report filed after the Battle of the Alamo, Mexican Col. José Juan Sánchez Navarro included this map of the Mexican troops' attack on the San Antonio mission. It shows positions of cannons (R and V) and the pattern of approach General Cós's troops took (S) in the predawn assault. The chapel (B) of *San Antonio de Valero* is now the only remaining portion of the Alamo structure. Courtesy of the Barker Texas History Center, the University of Texas at Austin.

Francis Johnson had assumed command of the Texas troops in San Antonio, but he was persuaded by Dr. James Grant to set out with a contingent to follow Grant to Matamoros to seize the contested lands. Grant promised them all the loot they could capture as their reward. When Houston got wind of the scheme, he cautioned that it would only provoke a harsh response from the Mexican government. But the Consultation's council paid no heed, commissioning Colonel James Fannin, then headquartered at Goliad, to lead the expedition, and giving Jim Bowie similar authorization. Although the expedition never materialized, Houston despaired of an army that would not follow him and, after Mexican agents had attempted to cause an uprising among the Cherokee Indians, he went off to East Texas to negotiate a peace treaty with Chief Philip Bowles.

In October Santa Anna determined that the time was ripe to sweep north to suppress this latest rebellion against his centralist policies. Fresh from quashing a revolt in Zacatecas, he moved north with some six thousand men. He crossed the Rio Grande in mid-February, intending to chase every Anglo from Texas.

The Texans in San Antonio were not prepared to fight such an army. Following Johnson's departure on the Matamoros scheme, Colonel James C. Neill commanded at San Antonio. He complained bitterly that Johnson had taken most of the men and nearly all of the supplies. Lieutenant Colonel William B. Travis arrived in January with only a few recruits and soon found himself in command, Neill departing on leave. With engineer Green B. Jamison,

Travis built up into a fortress the old compound of the San Antonio de Valero Mission, known familiarly as the Alamo. Bowie, instead of trekking off to Matamoros, arrived at San Antonio with one hundred volunteers, bringing their total combined command to about one hundred fifty men. They received additional help when David Crockett arrived from Tennessee with a handful of men. Travis and Bowie argued over command, but neither of them did as Houston wished: destroy the place and escape. Finally Bowie became ill, and Travis assumed full command. He wrote letters to everyone, but especially to Fannin, requesting aid. Fannin's five hundred men at Goliad might have been of some help if they had come, but Travis needed many more than that when Santa Anna finally arrived.

Santa Anna divided his army at the Rio Grande. He sent General José de Urrea on a southerly course to capture Johnson at San Patricio and Fannin at Goliad, and Urrea accomplished both tasks with little difficulty. All Anglo prisoners, except a few who managed to escape, were executed on Santa Anna's order.

Santa Anna moved north with General Joaquín Ramírez y Sesma's command and began a thirteen-day siege of the Alamo on February 22. Travis's pleas for help continued: "We consider death preferable to disgrace. . . . For God's sake and the sake of our country, send us reinforcements." His celebrated letter of February 23, 1836, addressed to all Americans, brought thousands from the United States, but all arrived too late to be of assistance to him. It did bring the entire male population of

33

Gonzales, thirty-five men, raising the small command to 185 men.

On March 6, 1836, the Mexican army stormed the Alamo. All of its defenders were killed during the battle or executed afterwards. Mrs. Susanna Dickenson, wife of Alamo artillerist Almeron Dickenson, was sent down the road to Gonzales to spread the news that the Alamo had fallen and that Santa Anna would sweep on to the Sabine River.

Santa Anna burned the bodies of the Alamo's defenders and regrouped before making good on his pledge. This delay al-lowed hundreds of troops to gather at Gonzales to await Sam Houston for the next move. Santa Anna had provided them with their battle cry: "Remember the Alamo! Remember Goliad!"

☆ Archie P. McDonald, professor of history at Stephen F. Austin State University, supplied these facts. You can read a stirring account of the Alamo in Lon Tinkle's *13 Days to Glory* (College Station: Texas A&M University Press, 1985). Also, a trip to the Alamo itself, run as a museum by the Daughters of the Republic of Texas, would be an excellent way to pursue an interest in this subject.

Establishing the Republic

When the eloquent Lorenzo de Zavala rose to address the Texan leaders gathered at the convention being held in the long, narrow log building, he began, "Mr. President, an eminent Roman statesman once said. . . ." Before he could say more, a fellow delegate broke in to advise that the convention give less thought to dead Romans and more attention to live Mexicans.

Indeed, as the constitutional convention convened at Washington-on-the-Brazos on the first day of March, 1836, its members had plenty to pay attention to. Santa Anna and his troops laid siege to William Travis and his volunteers at the Alamo. Gen. Martín Perfecto de Cós advanced on James Fannin and his men at Goliad. Stephen F. Austin and two other prominent leaders had been sent to Washington to seek aid. Perhaps most important, quarreling had plagued the ranks of Texas' civilian leaders almost since the moment the Consultation had adjourned the previous November.

At that earlier meeting, the assembly had declared itself loyal to the Mexican Constitution of 1824. Any acts of rebellion against the present government were acts in defense of that constitution. Texas was, and would remain, part of Mexico. Proper respect for the rights of states and recognition of Texas' status as a state itself, separate from Coahuila, was all the Texans asked.

So they had said. Now matters were more extreme, and the March convention had been called for the purpose of drafting a new constitution for an independent

As the wind of a "blue norther" swept through Washington-on-the-Brazos on March 2, 1836, Texan leaders gathered to consult on the Texas Declaration of Independence. Fanny and Charles Normann depicted the gathering in this painting. Courtesy of Mrs. Artie Fultz Davis.

Texas. The first matter at hand, then, was declaring Texas independent. This they did so quickly that ever after people have wondered whether George C. Childress, who wrote it, had in fact brought a draft with him. The convention signed the declaration on the second day, March 2, now celebrated as Texas Independence Day.

The declaration, written by a man re-cently arrived from Tennessee and signed by two former U.S. congressmen and a roomful of other immigrants from the United States, bore a strong resemblance to the U.S. document. It contained a long list of grievances against the Mexican government—including neglect, failure to guarantee freedoms that in fact were unique to the common-law tradition (freedom of the press, for example), and inciting the Indians against the settlers. It elaborated some philosophical principles of government and declared, unequivocally, that Texas was as of that moment a sovereign nation.

Once a nation, Texas needed a government. The provisional governing arrangements made by the Consultation had been woefully inadequate. For a few days before the Consultation met, Texas had had a Permanent Council, headed by Richard Royall, the Texans' first attempt to establish a government. The Consultation replaced this council with a governor, Henry Smith; a lieutenant-governor, James Robinson; and an advisory council. Bickering between Smith and the council quickly escalated to quarreling, and the council tried to impeach him. By the time the convention met in March, it was clear that a strong provisional government and a workable constitution were needed. The several Mexicans present were outnumbered by U.S. immigrants, and in any event the Mexican experience with constitutional government was only recent and had been thus far less than satisfactory. Again, then the Convention turned to the powerful nation to the east for a model. Fifteen days later, on March 17, the delegates had a constitution, one that would serve them until their admission to the United States some nine years later required its modification.

The new document's first article divided the branches of government, like that of the United States, into legislative, executive, and judicial departments and prescribed for each branch its functions and the qualifications for its officeholders. The constitution called for a president and a vice-president, a bicameral legislature, and a judiciary headed by a supreme court. This article also identified the nature of the government as unitary, rather than federal.

The second article enumerated the powers of the Congress, including the authority to levy and collect taxes, regulate commerce, coin money, establish post offices, declare war, maintain an army and navy or militia, and make "all laws deemed necessary and proper to carry these into effect." Article three gave the first president a two-year term but extended subsequent presidential terms to three years without the privilege of immediate succession. Other articles created a supreme court, identified specific presidential powers, established an *ad interim* government to guide the Republic until the permanent government could be established, and set out a Declaration of Rights. One curious article barred "ministers of the gospel . . . or priests of any denomination" from service in any executive or legislative office.

Richard Ellis, a delegate from Red River and president of the convention, led the delegates in signing the document. Following the Constitution's directions, the convention named an *ad interim* government, with David Gouverneur Burnet as president and Lorenzo de Zavala vice-president.

As the Convention adjourned, President Burnet faced many problems. Sam Houston, who in September would become the first elected president of Texas, had been named commander-in-chief by

36

the Convention and had left a few days earlier to rejoin his army. The Alamo had fallen, with no quarter asked or given. Ahead lay the Goliad massacre and the Runaway Scrape, shaky finances for the desperate new nation, strained relations among Texan leaders, and the need to control an unruly army. As they walked from that log structure into the March sunshine along the Brazos, one may well wonder whether the drafters of the new government felt elation at what they had accomplished or dread of what was yet to do.

⭐ This story of the founding of the Republic draws on materials furnished by Archie P. McDonald, professor of history at Stephen F. Austin State University. You can see a replica of the building where the founding documents were signed, and many other fascinating mementos of Texas history as well, at the Star of the Republic Museum, Washington-on-the-Brazos.

San Jacinto

William B. Travis's letters brought men to Gonzales, but until Sam Houston arrived from Washington-on-the-Brazos they had no leadership. He found 374 men there and learned that they had not heard the signal cannon fired each morning from the Alamo for the last five days. He dispatched Erasmus ("Deaf") Smith down the San Antonio road to reconnoiter and Smith returned with Mrs. Dickenson. The terrible grief of the women of Gonzales when they learned that all their husbands and sons had been killed along with the rest of the Alamo's defenders fixed a grimness upon every man there.

Houston realized that his small army, no matter how determined, was no match for Santa Anna's troops. Ordering Gonzales burned, he moved his force east to the Colorado River, where he intended to drill them and make a stand. Then the news of the massacre at Goliad caught up with the Texans, and Houston knew that even more troops would be joining Santa Anna. He moved again, this time to the Brazos River. News of the defeats at the Alamo and at Goliad and of Houston's retreat reached the civilian population and produced panic. People ran from their homes, leaving meals uneaten. Corn lay abandoned in cribs, and furniture too heavy to move farther was cast on the roadside. This Runaway Scrape was made more difficult because spring rains had swollen the streams and turned roadbeds into quagmires. "Our hardships began at the Trinity," Dilue Rose Harris remembered in an account published in *Texas Tears and Texas Sunshine*, edited by Jo Ella Powell Exley (College Station: Texas A&M University Press, 1985). "The river was rising and there was a struggle to see who

37

William Huddle's painting "The Surrender of Santa Anna" shows a wounded Sam Houston beckoning to the captured Gen. Antonio López de Santa Anna, while famous scout "Deaf" Smith strains to hear the proceedings. The original of this painting hangs in the state capitol. Photograph courtesy of the Daughters of the Republic of Texas Library, San Antonio.

should cross first. Measles, sore eyes, whooping cough, and every other disease that man, woman or child is heir to, broke out among us."

Santa Anna divided his army into three groups to pursue Houston and strike other Anglo settlements. General José Urrea continued along a coastal route to attempt to capture president David G. Burnet at Columbia; General Antonio Gaona moved northeastward to capture Nacogdoches;

and General Joaquín Ramirez y Sesma, flanked by the other two forces, pursued Houston. Santa Anna accompanied Sesma, sometimes in his advance with a smaller body, and soon he diverted Gaona to rejoin the center march. Santa Anna followed Houston's path to the Brazos River, where Houston had stopped to drill his men on the plantation of Jared Groce. Houston then moved farther east, leaving Moseley Baker's company to dispute the river crossing with Santa Anna. Santa Anna thought that Houston would try to escape to the safety of the United States but reasoned that he might still capture Burnet, who had moved the government to Harrisburg. He quickly advanced ahead of Sesma's main command with only five hundred men.

When Houston learned that Santa Anna had done this, he moved due east, taking no council with anyone. Many felt that they were being led away from battle, but Houston wrote his friend Henry Raguet on April 18 that he intended to fight. As Houston's lead reached a fork in the road, one way leading to Lynch's Ferry and the United States and the other to Harrisburg, Buffalo Bayou, and a showdown at San Jacinto, their commander gave no directions. The lead split the fork, but when some of the troops turned south, the others hastened to reassume their position in the march. Generations have speculated on whether Houston was thus led to battle by his men or, with brilliant psychological insight, allowed them to make the decision so that they would fight harder.

On the afternoon of April 20 the Texans reached the field and positioned the bayou to their back, the river to their left. The smaller Mexican force faced them a mile away across a rolling plain. An indecisive skirmish occurred about 4 P.M. Then, during the night, General Martín Perfecto de Cós arrived with five hundred men, making Santa Anna's force the larger army. During the morning of April 21 the armies faced each other, the Texans anxious while other leaders argued with Houston over whether or not they should fight, and the Mexicans drowsy from being up all night positioning Cós's men. Later in the afternoon Houston led about seven hundred men across the plain of San Jacinto, shouting for his men to hold their fire while a fife played "Will You Come to the Bower I Have Shaded for You?" for the march. His artillery—the "Twin Sisters," gifts from the city of Cincinnati—opened a hole in the Mexican line, and the Texans poured through. They caught the Mexicans by surprise. The battle lasted only eighteen minutes, but the Texans continued the slaughter of their fleeing foes for hours. The Texans lost two men in the action, and seven more died later. About thirty Texans were wounded. The Mexicans lost some six hundred men, and more than seven hundred were captured, including Santa Anna, who was discovered the following day attempting to escape to rejoin the larger body of his troops.

Houston had been severely wounded in the leg during the battle. Lying under an oak tree when Santa Anna was brought before him, he had to prevent the Texans from executing the Mexican president. Houston soon departed for New Orleans for medical treatment, leaving the job of negotiating with Santa Anna to President Burnet. By the time of the Treaty of Velasco, which they signed on May 14, 1836, Santa Anna had ordered all his troops to return to Mexico, and they surprisingly had obeyed. The Mexican president conceded independence and everything else demanded in return for his safety. Although his government later repudiated these concessions, the Battle of San Jacinto marked the end of the war and the beginning of the functioning, if struggling, Republic of Texas. The legacy of the dispute over Texas' boundaries would be for the United States to collect.

⭐ This information was provided by Archie P. McDonald, professor of history at Stephen F. Austin State University. There are several good biographies of the hero of San Jacinto; one you might particularly enjoy is by Marquis James, *The Raven: A Biography of Sam Houston,* which has gone through several editions. A monument and museum now mark the San Jacinto battlefield; a visit there can help you explore this important facet of Texas history.

Juan Seguín

Tejanos, or Mexican Texans, faced a dilemma in 1836: should they support the Texas insurgents, with whom they agreed on the issues of a decentralized government and the economic development of Texas, or should they remain loyal to their ethnic base and oppose the Anglos? Unable to be completely at home in either camp, they ultimately were cast out of both. Juan Nepomuceno Seguín, a natural leader in the group, personifies this dilemma.

Seguín, the son of Erasmo Seguín, was born in San Antonio on October 28, 1806, to an influential family. Life in Texas during his childhood was rugged and uncertain, even for one with his family's position and wealth. The province lay hundreds of miles from the center of Mexican cities. Disease and Indian attack haunted it. Texas was peopled by only twenty-five hundred settlers, most of whom lived around Nacogdoches, La Bahía (Goliad), or San Antonio. Survival required mastering the vagaries of frontier life, and the Seguín family had done that well.

Like others in the upper class of Mexican Texas, the Seguíns supported Mexico's liberal immigration policy of the early 1820s. Increased immigration from the United States meant the development of the local cotton economy and improvement of their family finances. One drawback to the immigration was that slavery, which they opposed, would have to be tolerated. Still, the Seguíns were prominent supporters of this program of economic enterprise.

Once the Americans arrived, Juan Seguín found other things besides slavery to offend him. The Anglo immigrants at Goliad and the new town of Victoria were notorious for acquiring property illegally, rustling livestock, and behaving arrogantly toward the native Mexicans. Their treatment of Tejanos alienated people like Seguín, who found themselves torn between the new economic opportunities the Anglos had introduced and the cultural submission they seemed to require. As tension mounted in the 1830s, Tejanos were in a quandary. Moreover, anyone who sided with the losers would surely find all property confiscated.

Though Jefferson Wright's 1838 painting portrayed Juan Nepomuceno Seguín as a Tejano hero of the Texas Revolution, Seguín later encountered hostility from some Anglo-Texans and was forced into exile in Mexico. Recent historians of the Texas Republic have re-evaluated Seguín's role and confirmed his contributions as an early Texas leader. Courtesy of the Texas State Archives, Austin.

When the crisis broke, Juan Seguín sided with the insurgents. Indeed as political chief of San Antonio in 1834, he anticipated the rebellion by providing strong leadership for Texas during the dispute over whether the state capital should be located at Monclova or Saltillo. He was credited with calling "the first strictly revolutionary meeting in Texas" to provide a provisional government during that dis-

pute. Although severely reprimanded for this action, he continued to oppose the centralizing efforts of the government of Antonio López de Santa Anna. By the time Gen. Martín Perfecto de Cós arrived in San Antonio in late 1835, Seguín had raised Tejano volunteers to fight against the Mexican army. The record he went on to compile in the war was nothing short of amazing.

Seguín's troops joined Stephen F. Austin at Gonzales in October to defend the cannon there and helped lay siege to San Antonio. Seguín fought with James Bowie in the skirmish at the Concepción mission, led foraging expeditions, and lured deserters from Cós's army to join the Texans. He participated in the siege of Béxar, and following the battle in early December, he helped William B. Travis obtain horses from the Mexican army.

In January, 1836, Seguín was commissioned a captain in the Texas cavalry and reported for duty in San Antonio. Sent out to seek reinforcements, he did not die with the Alamo's defenders in March. Instead, he joined Houston's men at Gonzales, where he was placed in charge of the rear guard to make certain that no family was left behind. Seguín aided Moseley Baker in slowing Santa Anna's crossing of the Brazos River, then joined Houston for the battle at San Jacinto on April 21, 1836.

A new dilemma plagued Seguín once Texas won its independence: Tejanos faced recriminations from vengeful Anglos who lumped all Mexicans together as the enemy. In the months after San Jacinto, many native Mexicans were banished from the homes and ranches to which they had the ties of generations. Seguín himself was promoted to lieutenant colonel and ordered to take over the military government of San Antonio. There, as more and more Anglos drifted in, he felt discrimination firsthand. The Tejanos looked to him for succor against Anglo insensitivity, and he was elected San Antonio's mayor in 1841, after having served in the Republic's congress, where he had worked for such measures as the printing of all laws in Spanish as well as English.

Ultimately, Seguín fell victim to a fate similar to that of many other Tejanos. Already the victim of a smear campaign by a faction of Anglo political opponents following his refusal to obey orders to burn San Antonio several years earlier, he was falsely accused of aiding Rafael Vásquez in his capture of the city in 1842. Seguín fled to Mexico to avoid assassination. In September of that year Santa Anna forced Seguín to accompany Adrian Woll's raid on San Antonio, and his participation confirmed many Anglos in their belief that he had been disloyal all along.

With Sam Houston's approval, he returned to Texas in the late 1840s, his fortunes in shambles. He managed to make small political gains, though only at the lowest governmental levels in Bexar County, where he was well known. In 1862, he returned to Mexico to fight in Benito Juárez's army against the French.

Until his death in Nuevo Laredo in 1890, his home alternated between Texas and Mexico. A victim of the changes he had helped to bring about, he demonstrated in his vacillation between dwelling places the dilemma of the Tejano revolutionary, who found himself with no home that truly welcomed him.

☆ Information on Juan Seguín was provided by Arnoldo De León, associate professor of history at Angelo State University. You can learn more about the dilemma of Mexican Texans after Anglos arrived in Professor De León's book *They Called Them Greasers: Anglo Attitudes toward Mexicans in Texas, 1820–1900* (Austin: University of Texas Press, 1983).

Houston and Lamar

For eight of the nine years the Republic of Texas existed, one of two men diametrically opposed in style and substance led the nation as president. Sam Houston, prohibited by the constitution from succeeding himself after serving as the first president of the Republic, held the office from 1836 to 1838 and then again from 1841 to 1844. Between his two terms, his archrival, Mirabeau Buonoparte Lamar, presided. In Houston's first term, Lamar served as his vice-president, but they quickly grew apart as they locked horns on every policy of the young Republic. Their personalities sealed their conflict.

Hard-driving, prickly, and often less

President Sam Houston had difficulty steering a peaceful course for the Republic of Texas in its relations with both Indians and Mexico. Courtesy of the Barker Texas History Center, the University of Texas at Austin.

than tactful, Houston had successfully led Texas' somewhat irregular army through a violent revolution. Reserved and diffident, a poet of some consequence—although his reputation in that regard was not an asset in the hurly-burly of Texas politics—Lamar had arrived in Texas just in time to share in the glory of San Jacinto.

An adopted son of a Cherokee chieftain, Houston had lived with the Indians as a young man in Tennessee and was proud of the name they had given him, "the Raven." As president he sought to honor treaties and discouraged attempts to encroach upon Indian lands. Lamar, on the other hand, as a newspaper editor in Columbus, Georgia, had enthusiastically defended President Andrew Jackson's Indian removal policies, and he brought those views with him to Texas. In 1839, having obtained evidence of a Cherokee-Mexican plot, he waged the Cherokee war and drove the Indians from East Texas. In 1841, at the battle of Plum Creek, near Seguin, his troops scored a major victory over the Comanches.

Sam Houston's goal was to get Texas into the American union as quickly as possible and turn the Republic's troubles over to a larger, more established government. Mirabeau Lamar dreamed of building an even larger empire. Houston, worried about the nation's debt and weary of war, sought to damp the conflict with Mexico. Lamar advocated campaigns against Mexico, expensive actions such as the Texan–Santa Fe Expedition, which the infant Republic could not finance. Instead of worrying about money, Lamar simply printed more, despite the resulting drop in its value.

Perhaps the conflict between the two presidents is typified best in their struggle over the location of a capital. Houston assumed office at Columbia, where he accepted the reins of government from interim President David G. Burnet, but he soon moved to a new community on the Buffalo Bayou named for him by its developers. While Houston deplored the climate and the prevalence of yellow fever there, he recognized that his support was based there. Lamar refused to serve in Houston. Before his term ended, he moved the capital to a new town on the Colorado

43

River named Austin. Lamar understood that his vigorous Indian policies were popular on the frontier. He also believed that the future population growth of the Republic would be concentrated in its western areas. Once re-elected, Houston, in his turn, refused to serve in Austin, claiming that it was too exposed to Mexican and Indian raids. He tried to move the capital back to Houston, but angry citizens of the new western outpost used a show of force to prevent the removal of the national archives. The capital stayed in Austin, and in 1844 Anson Jones put an end of sorts to the feud, when he assumed the reins of government.

Houston's administrations yielded a rather mixed record. He did gain an uneasy peace with Mexico, although it was more Mexican weakness than Texan resolve that allowed him to do so. His commitment to honoring treaties with the Indians was undermined by the Texas Congress's rejection of a treaty with the Cherokees and the subsequent aggressive policies of Lamar. His attempts to join the United States failed, largely because Texas would enter as a slave state. In his first term he did achieve U.S. recognition for Texas, but by the end of his second, annexation still eluded him—although it was to come, shortly, when victorious U.S. Democrats fulfilled a campaign pledge for the "re-annexation" of Texas.

Lamar, too, had a mixed record of successes and failures. Two of his legislative achievements, though, have had particularly lasting effects. Both were enacted in the 1839 session of congress and had the support of all political factions. The Home-stead Exemption Act, a legacy of Spanish law, guaranteed a homestead as well as the "tools and apparatus of a man's profession" against seizure for indebtedness. Passed to encourage farming and migration to Texas, the principle has been endorsed at every succeeding state constitutional convention and was the model for the U.S. Homestead Act of 1862. Also, the Education Act of 1839 set aside the proceeds from the sale of designated land in each county for the maintenance of "free public education." In accordance with Lamar's wishes, the same statute called for the establishment of a "University of the first class" and provided land for it, as well. Although he did not live to see it, the founding of the University of Texas in 1881 fulfilled Lamar's dream. The 1839 education act won him the appellation of "Father of Texas Education."

Perhaps the conflict between Houston and Lamar embodied the strains the new nation was under. Perhaps from the beginning the conflict could only be ultimately resolved, as the controversy over the state capital was, after annexation—when Austin was named capital, and the dispute with the Mexicans was taken on by the stronger United States.

⭐ Stanley E. Siegel, professor of history at the University of Houston–University Park, made this information available. A classic history of this period is William Ransom Hogan's *The Texas Republic: A Social and Economic History* (1946), released in paperback by the University of Oklahoma Press.

Academy-trained in Dresden, German artist Richard Petri immigrated to Central Texas with his family, who are portrayed in this barnyard scene by Petri. Courtesy of the Texas Memorial Museum, Austin.

German Immigration

In Texas, "nails grew overnight into horseshoes," Charles Sealsfield's *Cabin Book* told restless Germans in 1841. At home, life was made dreary and hopeless by political and economic repression; in Texas fertile soil, plentiful land, and freedom would fill life with opportunity. Opportu-

nity was a theme repeated in many a journal, travel account, and promotional brochure. In her journal, one early arrival described Texas as a strange landscape that inspired fear of the unknown mingled with a yearning to see what lay ahead. "I find that one is overcome with an amazing change; the farther one comes inland, the more civilization ceases. I don't know how it happens, but I have never been more content and in better health. I now have the courage to tackle any and all things and I know now that everything will take root."

And so they came. The German immigrants, filled with Old World expectations, founded beautiful settlements like Industry and Frelsburg. Then, in 1842 the Adelsverein, an immigrant aid society, sent Prince Victor von Leiningen and Count Joseph Boos Waldeck to Texas to seek grants for German settlement. Prince Carl of Solms-Braunfels, arriving in Galveston the next summer, prepared to receive the first of these immigrants. He purchased a tract on Matagorda Bay to use as a landing place and a staging point for their journey into the interior. Then he negotiated the purchase of lands for a permanent settlement on the Guadalupe River where it drops dramatically from the hills of the Balcones Escarpment.

Three shiploads of Germans arrived at Galveston in December, 1844, and proceeded down the coast to Matagorda Bay, the new port, which Prince Carl named Carlshafen (Carl's Harbor) and which was later known as Indianola. A warehouse and other facilities were erected, but there were no living accommodations for the weary immigrants. Although forced to camp temporarily on the open beach in winter weather, the first immigrants fared relatively well.

In a climate of international intrigue and chicanery, Prince Solms led them out in wagons and ox carts to the land he had secured for their settlement. On March 21, 1845, they arrived at a verdant woodland on the Comal River and established a town, naming it New Braunfels after the prince's home on the Lahn River. New Braunfels, the first colonial German village in Texas, quickly became a comfortable Old World town on the Texas frontier. Men worked together to build their homes, a church, and a fortress and to lay out streets.

Within a year, good prospects turned to bad. The United States went to war with Mexico, and money became scarce. New colonists were stranded on the coast when teamsters contracted to transport them inland were conscripted to haul weapons and munitions for the Texas army instead. Hundreds and hundreds of the hapless immigrants were buried in mass graves: a thousand died at Carlshafen alone. Once they could finally start, they faced a long journey, made more difficult by widespread fever and scurvy. Frequent rains mired the ox carts in the mud. The colonists were wet and miserable. Finally, within sight of their new home, they suffered another disappointment: the Guadalupe River was too high to cross. Several more died while they camped at the old ford, waiting for the flood to pass.

The survivors who finally reached Fredericksburg in 1846 faced Indian problems and the onset of a drought. By 1847, the Adelsverein was bankrupt, but a treaty negotiated with the Indians offered the Germans some security. Thus the colonization wavered between the good and the bad, between hope and despair. But the Germans looked everywhere for signs of promise. A teacher at Fredericksburg discovered in growth patterns of tree rings that periods of adequate rainfall alternated with shorter periods of drought. He predicted the imminent end of the dry spell. The settlers at Fredericksburg trusted and waited one more year, and it rained.

The daughter of New Braunfels' first pastor later described the early months in that community. "We had plenty of fish from the river, but not much meat. Ammunition was too hard to get. Milk and butter, beef and hog meat all came in due time, as did sweet potatoes and a few vegetables but no Irish potatoes for ever so long. We were hungry for fruit and had to be warned by our doctor against eating the fruit of the cactus. Parched barley and dried sweet potatoes were used when coffee gave out, and the men smoked all kinds of weeds when they couldn't get tobacco. Everything we could not raise for ourselves had to be hauled to us overland. Bales of unbleached cotton cloth had to come . . . from Mexico, and we had to dye it ourselves."

Despite these early hardships, New Braunfels grew steadily. Along with the hard-working farmers and craftsmen who made up the majority of the Adelsverein immigrants, minor nobles, gentry, and intellectuals also arrived. When a paleontologist-geologist, Dr. Ferdinand von Roemer, sent by the Berlin Academy first viewed New Braunfels in 1846, he predicted that the tree-filled market square would accommodate a city of twelve thousand inhabitants and that the town's fortunate location would ensure success.

By 1850, New Braunfels boasted three bakeries, other artisans, and several stores ranged along its dirt streets. Mrs. Kapp found the transition to the frontier settlement somewhat abrupt but admitted, "I envy all the young people of seventeen and eighteen years of age who come here. Even if they come with little or no cash, I firmly believe they can become independent within five to six years if they manage well."

In 1857, only twelve years after its founding, Frederick Law Olmsted praised the little city for its fine food. He lauded the "excellent soup" and particularly the "beautiful, sweet butter—not only such butter as I have never tasted south of the Potomac before, but such as I have been told a hundred times it was impossible to make in a southern climate. What is the secret? I suppose it is extreme cleanliness, and careful and thorough working."

In time the Germans came to occupy a good deal of the heartland of Central Texas and stamped their language and life-style upon the land. In time they adapted to the new environment, but they worked hard to preserve their heritage. They entwined their aspirations with backbreaking work and the promise of this new land to make their new home a place of opportunity and gentle fortune. The towns and villages and farms of the Texas Hill Country are evidence of their success.

☆ This overview of early German immigration was provided by Glen E. Lich, professor of history at Schreiner College. If you would like to know more about the German colonists, you might read *German Seed in Texas Soil* by

Terry G. Jordan (Austin: University of Texas Press, 1966) or, for a view of the distinctive lives of German Methodists in Mason County, the delightful book by his father, Gilbert J. Jordan, *Yesterday in the Texas Hill Country* (College Station: Texas A&M University Press, 1979).

Comanche — "Those against Us"

They called themselves Nermernuh, "The True Human Beings," but they were known to their enemies, the Utes, as Kohmahts, "Those against Us." Koh-mahts they were, with slight variations on the name, to the European explorers, missionaries, settlers, and soldiers with whose empires they collided in the mid-eighteenth century. They remained the Europeans' bitterest antagonists until their virtual destruction by the end of the third quarter of the nineteenth century. They were the Comanche Indians.

With their Kiowa allies on the South Plains, the Comanche were magnificent horsemen and warriors, who evaded the ancient dream of total Spanish conquest of North America, blocked the French advance into the Southwest, harassed the Mexican frontier, and delayed the advance of the Anglo-American frontier in Texas for almost sixty years.

Surprisingly perhaps, considering how hard they fought for the land, the Comanches were relative newcomers to what is now Texas. The very Spaniards whose nemesis they were to be provided them the means to become lords of the prairie: the horse. Through the seventeenth century, the Comanche were but a weak tribe of hunters and gatherers, allowed by their larger and more powerful Indian neighbors to forage over the eastern flanks of the Rocky Mountains in present-day Colorado, where the land offered little worth the taking. Everything changed when the Comanche began to acquire horses from tribes to the south, who in turn had acquired them from the Spaniards.

As they learned to use the horses, they began to grow in numbers and power. Now they could follow the buffalo out onto the Great Plains and south across the Red River. Now they could drive the Apache, Pawnee, Wichita, Waco, and other native nations out before them. In only a few decades Comanchería encompassed an empire from present central Kansas to Austin and from Oklahoma City to Raton Pass.

From 1758, when a war party attacked San Sabá Mission, until the Spanish army withdrew following Mexico's successful revolution in 1810, bands of Comanche warriors continually challenged and defeated the forces of the crown. The young Mexican Republic, weakened by decades of colonial misrule and revolution, was then almost totally at the mercy of raiding horse Indians. Surprise attacks and flight before the soldiers could regroup gave the

George Catlin was among the few non-Indian artists to visit and sketch the Comanches during their reign of power on the western plains. This drawing of these skilled horsemen depicts a favorite Comanche feat: hanging low from a galloping horse for cover. Illustration from George Catlin's Letters and Notes on . . . the North American Indians, vol. 2 (1841).

Comanche tactical superiority, which was bolstered by the strength of their commitment.

Stephen F. Austin's Anglo colonists at first were left strictly alone by the Comanche, who saw in them neither threat nor profit. As more and more Anglo pioneers pushed north and west of the original Texas settlements, however, conflict became inevitable. On May 19, 1836, several hundred Comanche warriors attacked Fort Parker, a stockaded community of eight or nine families near the headwaters of the Navasota River. After approaching the fort under a white flag, the Indians demanded one of the settlement's cows. When he refused to hand it over, they murdered young Benjamin Parker at the gates. Then, shouting war cries, the mounted warriors dashed into the stockade, where they cut down Samuel Frost and his young son. Elder John Parker, patriarch of the clan, and his wife attempted to flee, but they were ridden down. Parker died quickly, but Mrs. Parker was pinned to the ground with a lance, tortured, and left for dead. In a few minutes of bloody horror five men and two women were killed, several other women savagely wounded, and two young women and three small children carried away. One of the captives, Rachel Parker Plummer, saw an infant son, born in captivity, tortured to death before her eyes. In her eloquent memoirs written after her rescue, she cried out, "Surely, surely my poor heart must break."

Among the captives was the nine-year-old Cynthia Ann Parker, who, after a brief period of abuse, was adopted into the tribe. She quickly learned the Comanche language and came to ride as well as her new family and friends. Renamed Naduah, she became the wife of Peta Nocona, an important warrior, who eventually would lead his own band. Their son, Quanah, became the last great chief of the Comanche and led them in their final bitter struggle against his mother's kin. Cynthia Ann was recaptured in 1860 and returned to the Parker family with her daughter, Prairie Flower. She had long before become totally Comanche in her own mind and could not respond to the Anglo-American

civilization. Attempts to escape to her tribe failed. Her daughter soon succumbed to the white man's diseases, to which she had no immunity, and Cynthia Ann followed her in death shortly thereafter, in 1864.

The plight of the Comanche was not unlike that of Cynthia Ann. Faced with a culture they did not understand—and had no reason to want to understand—threatened by the extermination of their food staple, the buffalo, and encountering an increasingly skilled military resistance, the Comanche succumbed. In 1867, the Indians signed the Treaty of Medicine Lodge Creek and agreed to move to a reservation in Indian Territory. Although they continued raids from their new base, the end was upon them. By 1874 the brave warriors who had thwarted the schemes of Spaniards, Mexicans, and Anglo settlers for over a hundred years, found themselves vanquished.

☆ Thomas W. Cutrer, associate director of the Texas State Historical Association, furnished this information on the Comanche Indians. You can read more about them in T. R. Fehrenbach's *Comanches: The Destruction of a People* (New York: Knopf, 1979).

Annexation

The Lone Star State, the twenty-eighth star in Old Glory's blue field, officially joined the American Union on December 29,

1845, a little short of ten years after Texas won independence from Mexico. Few in Texas expected it to take that long. Some

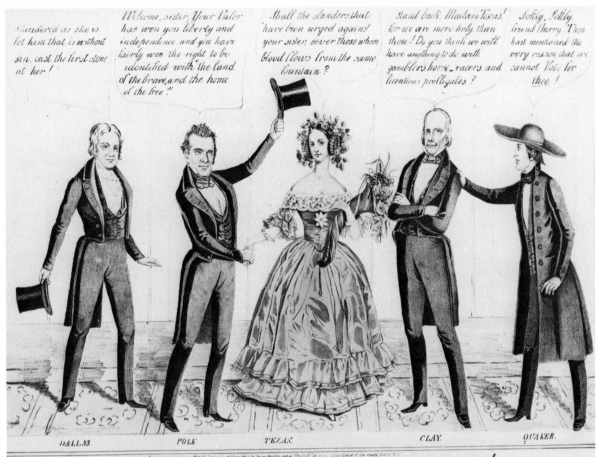

This 1844 political cartoon indicates the controversy Texas annexation raised in the United States. Democratic presidential candidate James Polk and his running mate George Dallas favored annexation, while Whig candidate Henry Clay resisted it through most of the campaign. Despite the best efforts of Virtue (depicted here as a Quaker) and his supporters' sentiments, Clay wavered on annexation in the end. His indecision contributed to his defeat. Courtesy of the Dallas Historical Society.

Americans, particularly southerners, had coveted Texas since the Louisiana Purchase in 1803, when the acquisition of the land adjacent to it made it the next logical step in their march toward the Pacific Ocean.

Although all Americans who came to Texas legally before the Revolution did so with the understanding that they were changing their citizenship, many cherished the thought that they would someday be reunited with their former country, and some probably participated in the revolutionary movement in the hope of eventual annexation. Nearly all of them continued to hold American rather than Mexican attitudes, particularly in matters of human and civil rights, and most never accepted the fact that those matters were different under Mexican rule. They cate-

51

gorized a system that was merely different as "wrong."

After the Revolution, when the Texas population had been enlarged dramatically by recent immigrants who had not participated in the Mexican colonial period, most evidently believed that annexation to the United States was a foregone conclusion. On the day they voted Sam Houston into office as the Republic's first president, they also voted 3,297 to 91 that Texas should seek annexation immediately. Houston did so as rapidly as possible in the hope that the larger, established government would save Texas from a new invasion by the Mexican army, Indian raids, and its financial troubles — in short, from its own weakness.

Houston's offer, which most Texans expected would be accepted, met with resistance in the United States, particularly in the Northeast and from abolitionists everywhere. Former president and now Representative John Quincy Adams led the fight against admitting an additional slave state to the Union, and particularly against Texas' joining it. To President Andrew Jackson, slavery was an economic matter, not a political one, and should not have figured in the decision. However, his handpicked successor, Martin Van Buren of New York, opposed annexation, and Jackson bowed to Van Buren's request not to compromise his administration by admitting Texas before he had a chance to establish himself in office. The best Jackson could do was to act on a congressional resolution that permitted him to extend diplomatic recognition to Texas. The Texans felt rebuffed, not only because their offer to join the Union had been rejected but also because Jackson sent only a charge d'affaires, not a minister, to represent the United States in Texas.

In conversations with President Van Buren, agents from Texas stressed the benefits for the United States if Texas joined the Union. Trade between the states would increase; Texas could enable the United States to satisfy the British demand for cotton; and the United States would obtain a naval presence in the Gulf of Mexico through Galveston's port facilities. Despite these advantages, Van Buren was cold to the proposal. He cited U.S. treaty obligations to Mexico, which opposed Texas independence, and he was sensitive to antislavery objections to annexation. Texas' proposal remained open for two years; then in 1838 an embarrassed Houston instructed his agents on the Potomac to withdraw it.

Houston's successor, Mirabeau B. Lamar, had no intention of joining Texas to the United States. Instead, he envisioned advancing the Republic's claims westward into New Mexico, perhaps all the way to the Pacific Ocean; so during his three-year term the question was not reopened. Lamar concentrated on winning the recognition of world powers, especially England and France, and also increased efforts to force Mexico to recognize Texas' independence.

When Houston regained the presidency in the election of 1841, he was ready to try again. That same year the death of President William Henry Harrison brought his vice-president, John Tyler, to the top

U.S. office. Tyler, a Virginian committed to annexation, resumed negotiations with Texas, partly out of alarm at potential British influence there.

A treaty drafted and sent to Congress in 1844 included Tyler's justification: Texas was "in a state of almost hopeless exhaustion, and the question was narrowed down to . . . whether the United States should accept the boon of annexation upon fair and even liberal terms, or, by refusing to do so, force Texas to seek refuge in the arms of some other power. . . ." The abolitionists, still led by Adams, remained unswayed. Their opposition, coupled with fears of war with Mexico, prevailed; the Senate rejected the treaty by a vote of 35 to 16.

Now the issue seemed dead for certain. Even some southern senators had voted against annexation. The new Texas president, Anson Jones, who would later style himself the "architect of annexation," let it be known that Texas had lost interest in joining the American Union and moved toward a closer relationship with Britain. This alarmed leaders in the United States, particularly in the Democratic party, who introduced the "re-annexation" of Texas and the "re-occupation" of Oregon into their electoral platform. Their candidate, James K. Polk of Tennessee, enthusiastically supported the measure. Henry Clay, the Whig nominee, conditionally endorsed annexation—if it could be done without giving offense to Mexico. A third-party candidate, the Liberty party's James G. Birney, adamantly opposed annexing slave territory.

Expansion proved more popular with the voters than with the Senate, and Polk won the election. A Texas bill was then rapidly drafted in Congress, even before Polk's inauguration. The legislation was framed as a joint resolution, which required only a simple majority vote in both branches of Congress, rather than as a treaty, which would require a difficult two-thirds majority in the Senate.

Three conditions were offered Texas for admission into the union. First, the United States reserved the right to "adjust all boundary questions," which would mean setting the boundary at the Rio Grande. Second, Texas would retain title to its public lands and apply the proceeds from the sale of those lands to the Republic's indebtedness. Finally, Texas reserved the right to divide itself into as many as five states—a right never yet exercised, of course.

In a last-ditch effort to keep Texas free of the American sphere, the British persuaded Mexico to recognize the independence of Texas if the Republic would pledge not to annex itself to the United States. Jones offered both propositions to the Texas Congress and to a special convention, and both overwhelmingly accepted the offer of annexation. A new state constitution was drafted at a convention in October, 1845, and, when the U.S. Congress accepted it on December 29, 1845, the Lone Star joined twenty-seven others in the Stars and Stripes. Texas was a state in the Union.

☆ Facts about Texas' efforts to join the Union were supplied by Stanley E. Siegel, professor of

53

history at the University of Houston – University Park. If you are interested in learning more about the "architect of annexation," Herbert Gambrell has written *Anson Jones: The Last President of Texas* (Austin: University of Texas Press, 1964).

Legacies of War

War between Mexico and the United States seemed inevitable in April, 1846, as armies from the two nations stood poised across the Rio Grande from each other. Behind them lay two nations hungry for fertile land and protected seaports. Behind them also lay two centuries of competition for territorial possessions in North America. Americans and Texans continued the English tradition of contesting lands held by Spain and Mexico, and Mexicans became heir of Spanish efforts to guard their northern frontier against the ambitions of their neighbor. The Texas Revolution, in a very real sense, shoved Anglo-Americans and Hispanics along the path toward the last major confrontation for control of the Southwest; the annexation of Texas to the United States provided the spark for the explosion of war.

From almost the moment Santa Anna signed the Treaty of Velasco in 1836, the Mexicans had threatened war if Texas were declared part of the American nation. In rhetoric still refusing to accept the independence of Texas, Mexico had come in fact to a kind of truce with the Texans, although raids north of the Rio Grande continued into the decade of the 1840s. When Texas was at last annexed by the United States, Juan Almonte, the Mexican minister to the United States, left Washington in protest. In response to this and other "insults"—and hungry for the vast Southwest—President James K. Polk sent American soldiers under the command of General Zachary Taylor to the Nueces River in South Texas; the Mexicans posted General Mariano Arista along the Rio Grande. Since patrols from both armies scouted the land between the rivers, a clash was inevitable. The first came on April 24, 1846, when sixty of Taylor's men ran into a Mexican brigade. Arista then attacked a bivouac commanded by Major Jacob Brown across the Rio Grande from Matamoros, and Taylor reinforced Fort Brown (later Brownsville). Thus both sides could claim that they had been fired upon on their own soil.

After two further battles on what Americans considered to be their soil—at Palo Alto and Resaca de la Palma—President James K. Polk signed a resolution declaring a state of war. Events would prove that neither nation was well-suited to wage war at the time, but Polk was eager to open Northwest Mexico to U.S. citizens.

Within a year, U.S. troops occupied Matamoros, Reynosa, and Saltillo, among

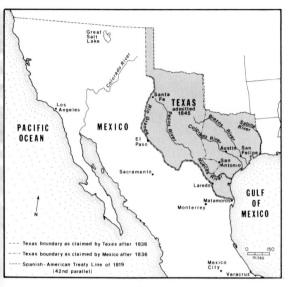

Following U.S. victories in Mexican territory and the capture of Mexico City, the United States forced Mexico to accept the 1848 Treaty of Guadalupe-Hidalgo and relinquish claim to most of its northern territory. That loss has long influenced U.S. relations with Mexico. Map by Jan Gaudaen, Austin.

several key sites, fought off Santa Anna's army at Buena Vista, and took Mexico's northwest coast (now California). General Winfield Scott landed his troops at Veracruz on the Gulf Coast in March, 1847, and moved inland toward Mexico City. Six months and several rugged battles later, Scott's army captured the capital city, signaling the end of the costly war.

By the terms of the Treaty of Guadalupe Hidalgo, ratified in March, 1848, the Texas-Mexico boundary was set at the Rio Grande, and Mexico surrendered all claims to Texas. Mexico also ceded other territory that later became the states of California, Arizona, New Mexico, Nevada, Wyoming, Utah, and Colorado, about one-quarter of the continental United States, in return for $15 million and the assumption of Mexican debts.

The war was over, but its importance would not be fully grasped for years. Acquiring lands well endowed with valuable natural resources and superior seaports assured Texas and the United States of a future filled with affluence and power. Conversely, the loss of the northern frontier seriously diminished Mexico's hopes for becoming a prosperous nation. Viewed in that light, the alteration of the border shaped the destiny of each country.

Moreover, moving the boundary caused a profound rift in cultural heritage. Some one hundred thousand people of Mexican origin who lived north of the Rio Grande were absorbed into U.S. society with the signing of the Treaty of Guadalupe Hidalgo. That document provided for the protection of their properties, religion, and civil rights, but neither the U.S. government nor American society lived up to that commitment. In effect, Mexican Americans became strangers in their homeland, as waves of Anglo immigrants overwhelmed them in key parts of the Southwest. Mexican Americans suffered discrimination in Texas, when the newcomers encroached upon their lands and came to dominate local politics. Violations of civil rights occurred, and contempt for Mexican culture dominated some parts of Texas society.

The tensions introduced by revolution and war were heightened by the role some Texans played in the war of 1846–48. More than eight thousand Texans fought

55

as volunteers in the war, led by Governor James Pinckney Henderson, who took leave from his office for the purpose. The Texas Rangers serving with Taylor and Scott earned the epithet "Diablos Tejanos" (Texas Devils) for their viciously competent fighting, and this reputation would add to the legacy of bitterness and mistrust.

This legacy of conflict engendered by the Texas Revolution and the war with Mexico lived on well into the twentieth century, as Texas continued to grapple with a dual heritage.

☆ Information about the Mexican War was provided by Oscar J. Martinez, professor of history at the University of Texas at El Paso. If you would like to read more about this sometimes controversial war, see Otis A. Singletary, *The Mexican War* (Chicago: University of Chicago Press, 1960).

Towns in the 1850s

A tradition persists in Jefferson, Texas, that Jay Gould came asking for railroad subsidies. When the town leaders, satisfied with their steamboat prosperity, turned their backs on the railroad tycoon, he built his railroad around the town and placed a curse on Jefferson: "Grass will grow in your streets, and bats will roost in your belfries." This is merely a legend. The Texas & Pacific came through Jefferson eight years before Gould bought the railroad, and no visit by Gould to Jefferson before 1880 can be confirmed. Moreover, many newspaper accounts attest to the interest of the town leaders in attracting railroads, and minutes of the city commission show the approval of generous bond issues passed to attract railroads.

Before the railroads came to Texas in the 1870s, Jefferson, in Marion County, was the riverport supply point for the vast area to the west and the trade center to which produce was hauled in wagons. The only other port for Texans was Galveston on the Gulf Coast, some three hundred miles south of Jefferson.

Since 1844, steamboats had been delivering cargoes to this East Texas town by a water route from New Orleans. The route followed the Mississippi, Atchafalaya, and Red rivers to a point north of Shreveport, and then through Twelve-Mile Bayou to Caddo Lake and eastward along Big Cypress Bayou to wharves in downtown Jefferson. The waterway was first opened by Captain William Perry, when he brought the *Llama* to Jefferson.

The Big Cypress water route allowing steamboats to reach Jefferson was formed by the blockage of the Great Red River Raft, a log jam extending one hundred miles, from a point north of Shreveport to a point north of Natchitoches. The log jam that clogged the Red River backed up

Jefferson's prominence lasted only as long as river transport prevailed in Texas and ended when the railroads that brought prosperity to other regions of the state bypassed it. Courtesy of the University of Texas Institute of Texan Cultures, San Antonio.

water into the bayous and kept the water level high and navigable in the Big Cypress Bayou, but beyond that point, riverboat traffic was blocked most of the time. No ports could be developed on the Red River north of Shreveport.

Although an occasional steamboat made it north on the Trinity River to Dallas, that city, founded by John Neely Bryan in 1841, had to seek rail traffic to stimulate its growth. On July 16, 1872, the Houston and Texas Central arrived in Dallas, providing a north-south rail route. It was only through legislative shenanigans that Dallas became a station on the east-west route of the Texas & Pacific, though. The road was to have bypassed the town, but a Dallas County legislator introduced in Austin a seemingly innocent amendment to the railroad charter, providing that the tracks should intersect those of the Houston and Texas Central within one mile of Browder

57

Springs. The amendment was passed with no questions asked; only afterward did the other legislators discover that the springs were near the business section of Dallas and were a source of the city's drinking water. Dallas, the apparent successor to Jefferson as the trade center of Texas, lay on the blackland prairie 180 miles to the east.

The Texas & Pacific Railroad did reach Jefferson in July, 1873, but once it established depots in other northeast Texas towns, trade trips to Jefferson by wagon were no longer necessary. Jefferson began to decline from a peak population of 7,297 in 1872, when the town was the sixth largest in the state. Final removal of the Red River Raft in November, 1873, made the river no longer navigable and eliminated Jefferson's port capacities. Then a series of disastrous fires destroyed a number of key businesses. By 1880 Jefferson's population had declined dramatically, to only 3,260, giving it a ranking of only fifteen among Texas towns. Dallas, meanwhile, continued to grow and to secure its position as the trade center of northern Texas.

In contrast to the tradition of the Jefferson curse, Jay Gould is said to have placed his benediction on Dallas, predicting the city would reach a population of 150,000 during his lifetime. To make sure that the prophecy came true, Rhodes Baker, a Dallas attorney, organized the One Hundred and Fifty Thousand Club. But when Gould died in 1892, the population had not yet reached 50,000, so a new goal had to be set: to realize the desired figure by 1900. Finally it was done; the 1920 census for Dallas recorded 158,876 residents. Twenty-eight years after his death, the city celebrated the realization of Gould's prediction.

Today Dallas is one of the ten most populous cities in the United States, with a population of almost one million. Jefferson counts a population of twenty-six hundred. Industrious citizens of Jefferson, perhaps fearing the curse of grass in their streets and bats in their belfries, have restored landmarks and preserved the history of their town, which was once the metropolis of East Texas.

☆ This information comes from Fred A. Tarpley, professor of literature and languages at East Texas State University, who also wrote *Jefferson: Riverport to the Southwest* (Austin: Eakin Press, 1983). You can learn more about this once bustling river town in that book.

Blacks in Antebellum Texas

Did Africans explore in Texas before the Spaniards arrived? Some believe that they did. A settlement of exceptionally dark Indians greeted José de Escandón at the mouth of the Rio Grande when he led an expedition there around the middle of the eighteenth century. Villagers recounted a tale of the arrival by sea, many years be-

Theodore Gentilz painted this scene of a slave family at home in the San Antonio area. His depiction was based on an early photograph. Courtesy of Larry Sheerin, San Antonio.

fore, of black men, armed with lances and shields. Marriage with local Indian women had created a new tribe, one of the most influential in the area. Legend did not reveal how the men had crossed the sea, but the expeditions from Africa were probably Mandinka in origin.

More is known about the blacks who accompanied the Spanish explorers as guides, navigators, soldiers, and even settlers, from the earliest expeditions into Texas during the 1520s. The most important Afro-Hispanic explorer was the Moorish captive Estebanico, who accompanied Cabeza de Vaca on his odyssey through the Southwest, a valuable guide because of his scouting expertise, his fluency in Native American languages, and his reputation as a medicine man. Having determined to domesticate and colonize Mexico, including Texas, Spain introduced some eighty-eight thousand captive Africans, or slaves, into the region between 1595 and 1640. As the imperial grasp of Spain extended into Texas, blacks commonly served as soldiers in the presidios located near the missions. By the middle of the eighteenth century intermarriage between Africans, Spaniards, and Native Americans was widespread, and captivity had declined drastically.

When Antonio Gil Ybarbo established the village of Bucareli on the Trinity River in 1776, a black weaver who traveled with him taught his craft to the Spanish settlers. Black vaqueros worked on ranches near San Antonio; two were Pedro Ramírez and José Rosalio. By 1792, 34 blacks and 414 mulattoes were numbered among the city's population of 2,992. They spoke Spanish and used Spanish names. Some of the blacks owned land, and many were skilled artisans. Few remained in bondage. As Texas passed from Spain and Mexico to the Anglos, the free blacks and their descendants were no longer differentiated in census records.

After the U.S. purchase of Louisiana in 1803, the growing abolitionist sentiment in Mexico attracted a tidal wave of blacks, some free and some runaway slaves. When abolitionist Benjamin Lundy journeyed through Texas in 1833, for example, he mentioned in his diary visiting Felipe Elua of Bexar County. Elua, a well-educated black landowner whose family spoke French and Spanish, claimed to have resided in Bexar County since 1807. The opportunity for black immigrants from the United States to obtain their freedom reached its zenith under Mexican sovereignty.

One of the most remarkable immigrants was Tamar Morgan. Morgan, who settled in Brazoria County after coming to Texas in 1832, through her own labor purchased her freedom in 1834 and became an independent landowner. She later married Samuel H. Harden, another black landowner of substance. At midcentury two of the largest landholders in Texas were William Goyens of Nacogdoches and the family of Moses Ashworth of Jefferson and Orange counties. Goyens, a native of North Carolina, settled in Nacogdoches in 1820. Working as a freighter, land speculator, blacksmith, attorney, and interpreter, he amassed an estate of 12,423 acres by the time of his death in 1856. He also owned a few slaves. The Ashworths came from South Carolina and Louisiana with their white father and settled in San Augustine County during the 1830s. By 1845 the family owned 14,296 acres and 2,240 head of cattle in Jefferson County. Five years later, Aaron, one of Ashworth's four sons, owned the largest herd in the county, 2,570 cattle.

Henry Sigler, a free black of Galveston County, was a barber, musician, and fisherman who sold his patent for an improved sockdologer hook to two New Orleans businessmen for $625 in 1858. Jim Brigham of Hunt County purchased his freedom in the early 1850s and founded the village of Neylandville, named in honor of a benevolent plantation owner.

In 1836, though, Texas achieved independence and began almost immediately to deprive the blacks among them of theirs. That very year, Texas halted the legal immigration of free blacks, and in 1840, free blacks residing in Texas were expelled unless they were specifically exempted by the legislature. By 1850 the number of free blacks listed in the census had dwindled to 397, and it dropped further, to 355 in 1860. This decline resulted from legislation passed out of fear of a black insurrection.

Black slaves, on the other hand, increased in number over the period, since they functioned as the fulcrum of the Anglo labor system in Texas. Slavery remained scattered in Texas under Mexican sovereignty, the Mexican government firmly opposing it. Anglo immigrants often circumvented the law, however, by claiming that black slaves were indentured servants. By 1825 Austin's colony included 443 slaves among a population of nearly 1,800 persons. After Texas declared its independence in 1836, the numbers of slaves increased dramatically, from approximately 5,000 to over 11,000 in 1840, to almost 60,000 in 1850, and to a little less than 200,000 in 1860. At the start of the Civil War, slaves represented approximately 30 percent of the population of Texas.

The conversion of Texas into a major producer of cotton and corn during the antebellum period was accomplished primarily through the efforts of black workers, and black slave artisans achieved some local and regional renown for their expertise. A white planter, James Woorling, recalled "Uncle Dave" and "Aunt Julia" of Rains County: "Uncle Dave was an exceptional Negro. He was a natural mechanic, but could do carpenter work, blacksmithing, shoemaking, and many other things equally well. He was a good manager, frugal and industrious. . . . Aunt Julia, his wife did her part. She was adept at cooking and preserving, and knew how to cure meat. . . . They had a spinning wheel and a loom made by Uncle Dave himself, and they made all the cloth owned by the family. . . ." While farming and crafts were common occupations for slaves, historian James Smallwood has observed that "the majority of the cowboys in Texas by the 1850s were probably black." Black cowboys were found primarily in East Texas between the Trinity River and the Louisiana border.

Seeking freedom, many black captives rebelled or ran away to Mexico or to Native American settlements. John S. Ford estimated that more than four thousand fugitives, valued at $3.2 million, had escaped to northern Mexico by 1855. The problem of runaways became so prevalent that Sam Houston and others proposed a U.S. protectorate over Mexico to close this avenue of escape from slavery. Not only were the relations between blacks and Mexicans close, relationships between blacks and some Native American peoples were also good. In 1849, Chief Wild Cat led a band of 150 blacks and Seminoles from the Indian Territory to the Rio Grande area near Eagle Pass.

Most white Texans did not own slaves, and many who did so owned only a few. But most believed in the institution and were willing to fight a civil war to preserve it and the principle of state determination.

☆ Melvine Wade, lecturer in Afro-American studies at the University of Texas at Austin, furnished this information. For a comprehensive survey of the history of blacks in Texas, read Alwyn Barr's *Black Texans: A History of Negroes in Texas, 1528–1971* (Austin: Jenkins, 1973).

Texas was on the periphery of action during the Civil War, but the Rio Grande was important as a center of cotton trade and transport. In November, 1863, Union soldiers moved into Brownsville, causing many Confederate sympathizers there to flee to safety, as portrayed in this Illustrated London News *drawing. John S. "Rip" Ford later recaptured the town for the Confederates and held it until the war's end, though Union forces blocked transport at the river's mouth.*

Secession and Civil War

"Governor Sam Houston . . . Governor Sam Houston . . . Governor Sam Houston . . . ," called the clerk of the Texas legislature. Three times he summoned the state's chief executive to take the oath of allegiance to the Confederate State of Texas. Houston sat quietly in a room nearby and refused to move. Then he heard his friend and former associate, Lieutenant Governor Edward Clark, called forth to take the oath as interim governor pending regular elections to select new officers for the state under the Confederacy. Houston had worked hard to get Texas into the Union only fifteen years earlier, and he would not lead his state out of it now. The victory of Abraham Lincoln and the Republican party in the presidential race of 1860 terminated a half-century of growing sectional consciousness and a decade of wedges of separation that drove the Union apart when the six Deep South states enacted ordinances of secession and drove Texas, the most recent state to join the Union, to become the seventh state to leave it.

The path to secession and Civil War deeply divided the people of Texas. Although a majority of the state's citizens had deep family, economic, and cultural ties to the slaveholding South, many of her prominent citizens, including Governor Houston, Congressman Andrew J. Hamilton, and former Governor Elisha M. Pease, opposed secession. Following the withdrawal of South Carolina, Texas separatists called upon Houston to authorize the election of delegates to a secession convention. When he instead called a special session of the legislature, hoping to head off separation, the secessionists persuaded the state's county judges to call the election, and a secession convention began in Austin on January 28, 1861.

The Texas Secession Convention over-whelmingly endorsed separation by a vote of 166 to 8, subject to approval by a popular referendum. This plebiscite was held on February 23, and 46,129 Texans voted for secession while only 14,697 voted against it. Support for secession was particularly strong in East Texas—except, curiously, in Angelina County—and along the Gulf Coast. The convention had anticipated the outcome by sending observers, who after the vote became official delegates, to the gathering in Montgomery, Alabama, that formed the Confederate States of America.

Opposition to secession and to war was strongest in the clusters of counties in Central Texas occupied by recent German immigrants and in an area of North Texas peopled mostly by farmers from the Upper South or the North. Both were frontier areas, heavily populated by non-slave-holders whose cultural roots lay outside the Deep South.

The first elections in Confederate Texas placed Francis R. Lubbock in the governor's office. Lubbock raised troops and divided the state into military districts. In 1860 there were 92,145 males eligible for military service, and from 60,000 to 70,000 eventually entered the Confederate army. In the beginning there was a rush to enlist. Local enlistees would typically form a company under some sponsoring planter or wealthy merchant. These companies were combined into larger units such as Hood's Texas Brigade or Terry's Texas Rangers.

The Texas Brigade, first commanded by John Bell Hood and later by ten other generals, became Robert E. Lee's favorite shock troops in the war in Virginia. "My

Texans," as he called them, bore the brunt of many battles, and only a few remained at war's end. Terry's Texas Rangers, formally the Eighth Texas Cavalry Regiment, served primarily in the western theater. General Albert Sidney Johnston, the highest ranking field officer in the Confederate army before his death in 1862, was one of 135 general officers with Texas roots, although only Felix Huston Robertson was a native-born Texan.

Not all Texans favored the Confederacy. Governors Houston and Pease withdrew from public life during the war, and Houston died in Huntsville in 1863 before it ended. S. M. Swenson, the "father" of Swedish immigration in Texas, and James P. Newcomb, editor of the *Alamo Express,* were driven from the state. Edmund J. Davis, a district judge, recruited the First Texas Cavalry Regiment for the Union army, and former Congressman A. J. Hamilton fled to Washington, where eventually he was appointed military governor of Texas to begin the process of Reconstruction. Other Unionists, such as James W. Throckmorton, one of the eight delegates at the convention who had voted against secession, put personal feelings aside and joined the Confederate army, although most remained in Texas to fight Indians if they could.

The first military commander of Texas was Paul Octave Hebert, a brusque Louisianan who made many enemies. He soon was replaced by Virginian John Backhead Magruder, who remained in charge in Texas until near the war's end, although after 1863 Texas became a part of the Trans-Mississippi Department commanded by Edmund Kirby Smith. In 1863 Lubbock left the state to join the staff of President Jefferson Davis. Pendleton Murrah was elected to replace him as Texas' second and last Confederate governor.

Those who remained behind faced many hardships, particularly with so many men gone. Women took over the running of plantations and did without sugar, salt, coffee, writing paper, and many other comforts. One, Kate Stone, a refugee in Tyler who had had to flee her beloved plantation in Louisiana, called Texas the "dark corner of the Confederacy" because of its primitiveness and the privations of war. During the war, more than two hundred thousand slaves were shipped to Texas in the hope that this would keep them safe from confiscation; these large numbers added to the state's problems during Reconstruction.

Few battles were fought in Texas. Early in the war John R. Baylor led a force to the west that claimed Arizona for the Confederacy, and H. H. Sibley and Tom Green led another to New Mexico that was successful until defeated by Union General E. R. Canby at the Battle of Glorietta Pass. Along the coast Union blockade ships captured Galveston, but the island city was reclaimed by men under Magruder in 1862 and remained in Confederate hands until the end of the war. At Sabine Pass Lieutenant Dick Dowling and about forty other Irishmen from Houston foiled General Nathaniel P. Banks's efforts to gain access to Sabine Lake, where he planned to land soldiers on Texas soil. And in 1864 Confederates under Richard Taylor, including many Texans, stopped Banks's advance up the Red River at the Battle of Mansfield. The last battle of the American Civil War was fought in Texas at Palmito Ranch near Brownsville on May 13, 1865, when Confederates commanded by John S. Ford defeated Union forces attempting to capture Fort Brown. From Union prisoners, Ford learned that General Lee had surrendered at Appomattox Court House in Virginia more than a month earlier.

⭐ Ralph A. Wooster, who provided this information on Texas' role in the Civil War, is dean of faculties and Regents Professor of History at Lamar University. You can learn more about Texas during this period by reading *Texas in Turmoil* by Ernest Wallace (Austin: Steck-Vaughn, 1965).

Juneteenth

"In That Great Gettin' Up Mornin'" rang through the campground; the sounds of celebration and the smells of barbecue, the hand clapping and the dancing proclaimed that a party was under way. The setting was rural Texas, and the time was any June nineteenth after 1865. On that day in 1865 Major General Gordon Granger and a contingent of Federal troops arrived in Galveston to proclaim the American Civil War at an end and all wartime proclamations of President Abraham Lincoln in effect in Texas. This included his Emancipation Proclamation, which had been issued on January 1, 1863.

In his proclamation, President Lincoln had declared that all slaves owned by Confederates in rebellion against the United States on that date would thereafter be considered free of bondage. It did not confer citizenship upon the free blacks, and it did not affect many people immediately. It exempted all slaves owned by persons not in rebellion, including all of Missouri, Kentucky, Maryland, and Delaware, and it could not even be enforced immediately in the states that were in rebellion because of the continued presence of the Confederate army. But once and for all it did commit the United States to the abolition of slavery and joined this goal to the preservation of the Union.

Granger's General Order Number 3 declared that the 182,566 slaves owned by the 21,878 slaveholders in Texas in 1860, plus all the slaves who had been sent to Texas during the war for safekeeping, were no longer "property"; they were free at last. Thereafter the day of liberation was known in both the black and white communities as Juneteenth. Afro-American emancipation holidays in the North usually commemorate the date of the Emancipation Proclamation, but blacks in most southern states, including Texas, celebrate the date that emancipation became effec-

65

Gen. Gordon Granger's announcement of the Emancipation Proclamation freeing Texas slaves on June 19, 1865, came to be celebrated annually in Texas, with speeches, picnics, and music. Pictured here is a turn-of-the-century "Juneteenth" band. Courtesy of the Austin History Center, Austin Public Library (PICA 05481).

tive for them. This differs from state to state, and Texas' Juneteenth is the latest on the calendar.

While emancipation did not mean full citizenship—this awaited the passage of the Fourteenth Amendment to the U.S. Constitution in 1868—blacks did enter a new relationship with whites and with their state and national government. This ushered in an era of jubilee, a pervasive mood of optimism that influenced black music, dance, and socializing. It also meant

that blacks would be registered to vote under the army's implementation of the Reconstruction Acts of 1867, and they held a few elective offices following the organization of the Radical Republican government. It would have been unthinkable not to celebrate such significant gains.

The annual parties varied from community to community, but Juneteenth celebrations typically included four elements: a midmorning parade, a noon commemoration service, a picnic and recreational activities in the afternoon, and a party in the evening, which might continue throughout the night. Since most blacks were Baptists or Methodists, their churches often served as the central organizations to plan a Juneteenth party, but schools, Masonic lodges, and, in later years, businesses, fraternities, and sororities also helped with the celebrations. Most blacks were given the day off from work for their party.

A parade usually began the day's festivities. It would follow a route through the heart of town and conclude at the commemoration site, usually a church, a school, or some other public meeting place. Large crowds of spectators of all ages, including representatives of the community's white population, would gather to hear band music and speeches. These orations reminded the audience of the significance of emancipation. There would be prayers of thanksgiving to God for the day itself and all it meant and for the living and the recently dead. Jubilee songs such as "Free at Last" and "In That Great Gettin' Up Mornin'" re-created the joy of attaining freedom. Patriotic songs were sung to affirm the newly won citizenship of the black community. A sermon by a preacher or a speech by a political officeholder or educational leader lauded Lincoln and his role as the Great Emancipator, praised the Union, or perhaps, in later years, addressed such subjects as a community project. It was customary to read Granger's declaration of freedom for Texas blacks. Always the highlight of the service was the testimony of former slaves about their lives before and after their deliverance.

After the commemoration service, the crowd gathered at a local park, usually on the edge of town, for a picnic and games of various kinds, including highly competitive baseball games, horse races, stunt riding, and rodeos. The preparation and sharing of food remained the principal attraction for most. Often local merchants, politicians, or patrons—white and black—donated pork or beef. The men usually barbecued the meat while the women prepared fried chicken, potato salad, sweet potato pie, peach cobbler, homemade ice cream, and "glassade," a blend of shaved ice, sugar, and fruit syrup. Red and orange "soda water," or pop, added liquid refreshment to the menu, and often alcohol would be present as well. The meat was shared by all, but usually the rest of the fare was prepared and shared by extended families. After dinner the celebrants danced to the music of the fiddle, banjo, or piano.

Juneteenth became firmly entrenched in nearly every Texas community that had a population of former slaves. For example, as early as 1872 Harris County had established an annual celebration of freedom. Under the leadership of the Reverend Jack Yates of the Antioch Baptist Church, the black community in Houston raised a thousand dollars and purchased a ten-acre site for the party. Renamed Emancipation Park, the site had a baseball field, dining pavilions, and a bandstand. It proved a special place for celebrating family values and for family reunions, and Juneteenth became a favorite time for the gathering of black families.

Juneteenth was celebrated by Texas blacks with the support and cooperation of white employers and patrons until well

67

into the twentieth century. It was less celebrated during the 1950s, 1960s, and 1970s because of several factors, including the refusal of some blacks to be associated with a reminder of slavery and because of the withdrawal of support by much of the white community in retribution for civil rights activism. Juneteenth has experienced a resurgence of popularity in the black community in recent years, to good effect: it reminds all Texans of the joy of freedom.

☆ This view of Juneteenth celebrations comes from Melvin Wade, lecturer in Afro-American studies at the University of Texas at Austin. To read more about black history after the Civil War, you could read James M. Smallwood, *Time of Hope, Time of Despair* (Port Washington, N.Y.: Kennikat Press, 1980).

Indian Wars

"If I could build a wall from the Red River to the Rio Grande so high that no Indian could scale it, the white people would go crazy trying to devise a means to get beyond it." Years later, Noah Smithwick, who had helped Sam Houston negotiate a treaty with the Comanches, attributed these words to Houston. Whether he really said them or not hardly matters. He could have and been accurate—for in the clash of Indian and European cultures the stakes were nothing less than the conquest and domination of central and western Texas.

The two ways of life were incompatible; one or the other had to leave the plains. The Plains Indians depended on buffalo for sustenance and required large numbers of free-ranging herds to hunt enough to eat. The Anglos by the 1870s sought buffalo for profit and land for settlements. They hunted the buffalo to the point of near-extinction, and they used the land cleared of the buffalo for farms. Conflict between two such different cultures could be resolved only by the total dominance of one people or the other. Although the Anglos' technology and greater numbers made the outcome inevitable, the courage, skill, and tenacity of the Comanche made the contest long and bloody and—for its first thirty years—seemingly uncertain.

Treaty after treaty proved meaningless. Pushed into Indian Territory in Oklahoma, the Comanche Indians used their reservation as a staging base for raids. With federal troops and Texas Rangers pulled back from the frontier during the American Civil War, the frontier itself was pushed back by the Indians. Killing or capturing scores of frontier settlers, the Comanche drove the line of Anglo settlement back from fifty to a hundred miles in North Texas.

With the end of the Civil War, however, United States soldiers and heavily armed buffalo hunters returned to Comanchería. The hide trade depleted the Indians' source of food, shelter, and tools, and the Fourth United States Cavalry under Col. Ranald Mackenzie followed the Comanche bands

The buffalo had provided food, housing materials, and clothing for Southern Plains Indians for decades. But by the 1870s, buffalo hides were valuable to non-Indians as well, and U.S. buffalo hunters were slaughtering the beasts to sell their hides, fueling the Indian Wars. Dodge City, Kansas (above), was a major shipping point for buffalo hides from the Panhandle region. Courtesy of the Kansas State Historical Society.

into their Panhandle stronghold and harassed them remorselessly with a series of unprecedented winter campaigns.

The two final battles that broke the Comanches' power forever were fought in the summer of 1874. The first occurred at Adobe Walls, a buffalo hunters' camp on the Canadian River, when some seven hundred Comanche, Kiowa, and Cheyenne warriors attacked a group of twenty-eight white hunters. The Indians were led by Quanah Parker, the son of a white cap-

tive woman and Chief Peta Nocona. Barricaded in the fortresslike buildings and armed with new Sharp's rifles, the buffalo hunters rained virtual destruction on the charging Indians. Indian morale was cracked on the second day of the fight, when Billy Dixon shot a Cheyenne from his horse at seven-eighths of a mile. After that, the Indians carried on only a half-hearted siege, and when additional hunters arrived, they fled.

Three months later, in the final and decisive encounter of the Indian wars, Mackenzie's hard-riding Fourth Cavalry discovered the remains of Quanah's band encamped in Palo Duro Canyon, where they probably felt the precipitous canyon walls afforded some safety. Under heavy fire, though, the troopers descended, routing the Indians and capturing the Comanche horse herd and great quantities of robes, blankets, food, and tipis. Although most of Quanah Parker's followers escaped, the brutal winter of 1874 forced them to abandon North Texas for the Oklahoma reservations.

Quanah Parker later became a wealthy stock raiser and personal friend of President Theodore Roosevelt. Although allowed to return to the Panhandle for occasional hunting expeditions, never again were the Comanche powerful enough to take the warpath against the hated Tejanos.

☆ Thomas W. Cutrer, associate director of the Texas State Historical Association, made available this information on the Indian wars in Texas. You can read a vivid account by one of the soldiers in the Fourth Cavalry: Robert G. Carter, *On the Border with Mackenzie; Or, Winning West Texas from the Comanches* (1935; reprint, New York: Antiquarian Press, 1961).

Reconstruction and the Constitution

Does Texas need a new Constitution? This question was debated heatedly in 1875–76 when the state's present constitution was written and adopted, and it has been raised again and again since then. Former Republican Governor Edmund J. Davis, elected in 1870 with the support of the Radical Republicans who had written the 1869 constitution, represented the minority of Texans who said "No." Redeemer Governor Richard Coke led the majority who emphatically said "Yes!" The constitution the voters subsequently ratified is still the basic frame of government for Texas after more than a century. Ironically, the controversy over revising or even rewriting the constitution is perennially with Texans.

Texans wrote their first constitution for the Republic in March, 1836. They adopted another one when they joined the United States in 1845 and amended that enough to serve during the Confederate years. They tried to amend it back again under President Andrew Johnson's plan of Reconstruction, but their proposals were not far-reaching enough for the U.S. Congress. Therefore, in 1868 Texans wrote a new constitution to meet requirements of the Radicals in Congress to regain admission to the Union. This constitution granted too much power to the governor and allowed the legislature to spend too much money to suit most Texans, so by 1876 a clamor had arisen for a new basic document.

The Constitution of 1876 represented a political reaction to the alleged excesses

An 1873 Republican newspaper ridiculed Democratic hopeful Richard Coke in this political cartoon in which Coke and his running mate, Richard B. Hubbard, are sketched as dogs seeking the Texas gubernatorial "bone." In 1874, Coke won the election for governor, replacing the controversial Republican Reconstruction governor, E. J. Davis. From the Daily State Journal, Austin, October 4, 1873.

of Radical Reconstruction, including the burning of Brenham a decade earlier. Most Texans resented Governor Edmund J. Davis's administration, especially his legislative program enacted by the Twelfth Legislature. The "Obnoxious Acts," as many called them, created a state police and militia under the governor, empowered him to fill all vacancies in office, and allowed him to designate an official newspaper. The Radicals also increased the pay of most officeholders and enacted programs voters considered too expensive. Several acts were even passed by the legislature while eight members of the Democratic opposition were held under arrest. Davis also maintained the right to suspend the writ of habeas corpus. Many of the acts of the Radicals were responses to the lawlessness of the era, but most Texans resented them just the same.

When Davis lost his bid for reelection to Coke, he attempted to maintain power by a legal technicality concerning the placement of a semicolon in his own election statutes, and the Supreme Court he had appointed upheld his claim. When the Democrats inaugurated Coke anyway, Davis appealed to President Ulysses S. Grant for troops to sustain his administration, but Grant refused them. Coke then called a constitutional convention to meet on September 6, 1875.

Besides Reconstruction, the most important influence in the convention came from the Patrons of Husbandry, an agrarian organization known familiarly as the Grange. More delegates represented this perspective than any other. Seventy-five of the ninety delegates were Democrats; the fifteen Republicans included six blacks. Important members included John H. Reagan, John Henry Brown, and Charles DeMorse. Following the lead of the Grange, the convention called for "Retrenchment and Reform." They lowered the salaries of all officials and reduced their terms of office. The governor's term was shortened from four to two years, and his powers were limited. Observers have said that the convention tried to leave the governor powerless, repose only necessary powers

71

in the legislature, and then keep the legislature from meeting. Indeed, it meets only every other year, and then for only five months. The convention nearly abolished the office of lieutenant governor, failing to do so by only two votes. Many did not want the state to spend money on public education, but eventually they designated revenues from public land and some land itself to support education, including higher education. So economy-minded were the delegates that they refused to hire a stenographer or pay for the printing of their proceedings. They did, though, support provisions for protection of the frontier, regulation of railroads, and development of immigration.

The constitution was adopted on February 15, 1876, by a vote of better than two to one, and, often amended, remains in effect today, despite an attempt to draft a new document in 1974. It resembles a time capsule in that it contains residues of previous constitutions. There are provisions that echo the Mexican Constitution of 1824 and certain land-law provisions from the colonial period. Survivals from the frontier era prohibit duelling and authorize the governor to ward off attacks by hostile Indians. There are provisions from the Constitution of 1845, which Daniel Webster characterized as among the best of American state constitutions. There are references to the Confederate Veterans Pension Fund and the American Civil War. Amendments reflect periods of economic growth and social change. The Constitution of 1876 holds much Texas history, but it does not necessarily reflect the way that Texas politics is actually conducted. For example, the office of governor is weak on paper but sometimes strong in practice because of the personalities of those who have held the positions, and the important and efficient activities of the party system are largely statutory rather than constitutional.

In spite of its many alleged defects and the fact that sometimes Texas government operates more in spite of its provisions than because of them, the Constitution of 1876 has been remarkably hearty and long-lived.

☆ This discussion of the Texas constitution and its roots is based on information furnished by Gilbert M. Cuthbertson, professor of political science at Rice University. Charles W. Ramsdell's classic *Reconstruction in Texas* (New York: Columbia University, 1910) can tell you more on the events leading up to the drafting of the 1876 constitution.

The Cattle Kingdom

"West of Kansas City there is no law; west of Dodge City there is no God" is a saying from the era of the Texas cattle drives. The Texas cattle industry was not always oriented northward, though. The first cattle were first brought to Texas with the Span-

Long cattle drives were rarities by the time Scribner's *published this drawing of a trail drive from Texas in 1892, and the cowboy had already become a stock character in popular fiction.*

ish *entradas* and religious missions. In 1746 José de Escandón's patrons established vast cattle and horse enterprises along the Rio Grande, and the resulting *charro* culture was soon transplanted across the river in the diamond-shaped area formed by the Gulf of Mexico on the southeast, the Nueces River on the northeast, the Rio Grande on the southwest, and hope on the northwest.

The hybrid breed that survived best there, the fabled longhorn, grazed this arid corner of Texas with only occasional interference or encouragement from vaqueros, or cowboys. When the Anglos came to Texas, most claimed they were cattle raisers, which entitled them to a larger portion of land; many, in fact, were, and others soon began to capitalize on the readily available resource. A few early drives, notably those by James Taylor White to New Orleans and, later, by others to other Mississippi River shipping points, proved less than successful because of resentment from farmers along the drive routes, especially after the spread of

"Texas Fever," a bovine disease carried by a tick parasite. So before the American Civil War the cattle industry essentially became a hide-and-tallow business.

During the Civil War many of the state's able-bodied men were called up to fight, leaving Texas crops and cattle alike untended. The cattle bred without thinning, and when the men returned to Texas they found three to four million head of cattle, largely in the area between San Antonio, Corpus Christi, and the Rio Grande Valley. Meanwhile, the North had increased its income and its population during the war. Northerners were hungry for beef, and they were able to pay for it. The problem was that the cattle were a thousand miles from market.

To solve the problem, Joseph G. McCoy, a twenty-six-year-old Illinois commission merchant, convinced the Hannibal and Saint Jo Railroad, a short-line road with connections into Chicago, to build a cattle town west of the settlement line. In this way Texas cattle trailed northward could avoid quarantine imposed because of the deadly typhoid tick they carried, to which they were immune but other cattle were not. McCoy then persuaded Texas drovers to turn their herds northward up a trail blazed by Jesse Chisholm toward the new town of Abilene, Kansas, where the necessary facilities for cow handling had been built. In addition to the railroad and holding pens, Abilene offered gambling halls, bars, and "soiled doves." Many Texas cattlemen took a chance on this man they had never met and sent their cattle to a town they did not know.

When a quarter of a million Texas cattle were trailed to a no-place called Abilene, on the first drive in 1867, the cattlemen found everything McCoy had promised. In the next twenty-three years, an estimated 10 million cattle were trailed north across Texas, the Indian Territory, and half of Kansas. Since the grass became better the farther north the cattle traveled, the steers often arrived at the railhead with more beef on them than when they left Texas.

Once Abilene became prosperous, its people sought respectability and began to frown on cowboy high jinks. To continue to attract the cowboys, the drives moved even farther west, especially to Dodge City. Cattle were also trailed into Colorado, Nebraska, Wyoming, and Montana; Montana proved a good "topping off" range. Eventually these newer territories and states became cattle kingdoms themselves, stocked mainly by descendants of the longhorn cattle originally trailed there from Texas.

The range cattle industry paid well for a while, but the advance of the railroad and barbed-wire fencing by farmers brought it to an end. The ranchers themselves contributed to its decline; they overstocked the range, destroying the grass. A miserable drought in 1885–86 coupled with one of the most severe winters in western history sealed the doom of the open-range kingdoms. That time was known as the year of the Big Die-Up. It not only drove many entrepreneurs out of the cattle business but convinced survivors that the days of uncontrolled breeding had to end. Ranching then became a business, and the free-ranging cowboy became a hired hand.

The cowboy was in some ways the

American equivalent of the medieval knight on horseback. Although his era was short, he has remained a worldwide symbol of a once-ample world, courage, and direct action. The cowboy's broad-brimmed sombrero with a high crown, high-heeled boots, rawhide lariat, spurs, silver-tipped western saddle with its big horn, and oversized stirrups contributed to his mystique. The gear was borrowed in large part from an Arab, Spanish, and Mexican heritage, the same heritage the longhorn grew out of. Although the gear was spectacular to the bench-bound Easterner, it developed for practical reasons, as did the roundup and other methods of tending cattle borrowed from the Hispanic past. Some of the terms for the gear are Hispanic, though many were corrupted by the Anglos who participated in the development of the cattle kingdom: rodeo; *la riata*, or lariat; *sombrero*; hoosegow for *juzgado*; buckaroo for *vaquero*; mustang, or *mesteño*, meaning a wild or untamed horse; and *remuda* for a relay of spare horses.

The longhorn and the cowboy, though they came from Mexico, became true Texans and one of the enduring symbols of the state. This can be seen in the number of institutions that have longhorn or cowboy in their title, from the University of Texas Longhorns athletic teams, the Dallas Cowboys, and all the high school teams named Cowboys scattered through the state, to a hundred Longhorn cafes and dry-cleaning establishments. The longhorn and his handlers seem to be an imperishable part of the state's tradition, no matter how urbanized or how far removed from the ranch future Texans may become. In the words of one poet: "Other states were bred and born / Texas was carved from hoof and horn."

☆ This information on the history of the Texas cattle industry comes from Joe B. Frantz, professor of history at Corpus Christi State University and professor emeritus of history at the University of Texas at Austin. Get a firsthand account of trail driving from Andy Adams, *The Log of a Cowboy: A Narrative of the Old Trail Days* (Lincoln: University of Nebraska Press, 1964).

Texas Rangers and Outlaws

To settlers whose ability to stay put on a rugged frontier depended on having the borders secure and the outlaws behind bars, the Texas Rangers were heroes worthy of the image the masked Lone Ranger later gave them. No problem Texans faced after the Civil War—and they faced many—was greater than crime and lawlessness, and in 1874 the Texas legislature took measures to deal with it. The Texas Rangers were born.

Thousands of defeated Confederate vet-

M. C. Ragsdale photographed this company of Texas Rangers loading their burros at a camp in Menard County in 1878. Courtesy of the Western History Collections, University of Oklahoma Library.

erans had flocked into the state—some returning Texans, but many refugees from eastern states. The farflung frontier was hard to protect from Indian raids; military rule and Reconstruction had created bitterness and disdain for established government. Economic conditions were grim, and, with criminals pouring into the state for "easy pickins," many already here turned to lawlessness, especially since law enforcement personnel were few and the chances of being apprehended slim. In 1876 Adjutant General William Steele compiled a list of "3000 known fugitives on the fringes of Texas."

To counter the problems, the Texas legislature in 1874 created two military forces to protect the frontier and suppress lawlessness. The Frontier Battalion, commanded by Major John B. Jones, was charged with controlling the Indians along the frontier. The Special Force of Rangers, headed by Captain L. H. "Lee" McNelly, the second group, held orders primarily to control banditry along the Rio Grande and general lawlessness in Southwest Texas.

In 1874 Captain McNelly and his Rangers drew their first assignment: the Sutton-Taylor feud, which had erupted in DeWitt County. They arrived at the county seat at Clinton on August 1. Subsequently, they brought an armed mob under control and, by means of an espionage system, individual courage, and out-and-out intimidation, arrested the principal lawbreakers.

By the end of the year McNelly was ready for reassignment. Governor Richard Coke sent him to the Nueces Strip, where for the next eighteen months the Rangers ruthlessly fought against cattle rustlers, Mexican bandits, and the forces of Juan Cortina, the "red robber of the Rio Grande." McNelly upheld the Ranger tradition of invincibility, toughness, and rugged determination and in the effort became known for his famous saying, "You can't stop a man who just keeps on a comin'."

When poor health forced McNelly to retire at the end of 1875, he was succeeded by Lieutenant John B. Armstrong. In 1877 Armstrong tracked down the notorious gunman John Wesley Hardin, who reportedly had killed as many as thirty men. With detective John Duncan, he traveled to Alabama to arrest Hardin, but the gunman had already departed for Florida. Armstrong and Duncan picked up his trail. Then, at a small station just outside Pensacola, Armstrong suddenly faced Hardin and his gang of four men alone and at close quarters. After one desperado fired a bullet through the Ranger's hat, Armstrong killed the man, pistol-whipped Hardin unconscious, and forced the other three to surrender. Armstong personified the Ranger mystique of "One Riot! One Ranger!"

Major John B. Jones was equally successful in directing a force of six companies in fifteen engagements during the first six months of their operation. He and his men were so effective that no Indian raids were reported in the latter part of 1875. Of all his exploits, however, Jones is best remembered for ending the career of Texas' most notorious train robber, Sam Bass. On July 18, 1878, Jones and three Rangers rode into Round Rock, just twenty miles north of Austin. An informant had told them that the town bank was going to be robbed. When the Bass gang came into town the next day to scout out the place, the Rangers surprised them in a running gun battle and wounded Sam Bass. Bass escaped temporarily, but the next morning he was discovered just north of town. He died later that day, July 20, 1878.

The swift and often fatal enforcement of the law by the Rangers restored order to the state. Most of the Anglo community regarded the Rangers as genuine heroes of their time, precisely because outlaws learned to fear them. As the frontier became more settled and law there became more institutionalized, the Rangers had to change their ways and adopt more constitutionally acceptable methods. They continued to be a hardy breed of Texans charged with protecting the citizens of the state long after they gave up their "shoot first and ask questions later" approach to law and order. But by that time, Hollywood fiction writers and other myth makers had capitalized on their history and elevated them to superhero status—a status that has not gone unchallenged by Mexican Texans, who had their own reasons to fear the Rangers.

★ These facts about the Texas Rangers were supplied by Ben Procter, professor of history at Texas Christian University. If you would like to learn more about this famous group of law enforcement agents, ask your librarian for a copy of Walter Prescott Webb's *The Texas Rangers: A Century of Frontier Defense* (Norman: University of Oklahoma Press, 1952).

In the summer of 1901, Texas Rangers joined local law enforcement officials to track down Gregorio Cortéz (seated center), a Mexican-American workman falsely accused of being a horse thief and murderer. Cortéz spent twelve years in prison before Mexican Americans convinced state officials to investigate his case and grant a pardon. Meanwhile, his encounters with the "rinches" or Rangers had become the subject of Tejano border ballads, some of which are still sung. Courtesy of the Barker Texas History Center, the University of Texas at Austin.

"Rinche, Pinche"

The Texas Rangers could never be taken lightly by their enemies, and their enemies included Mexicans crossing the border from the south, as well as Indians crossing any border to Texas, fugitives from the rest of the United States, and lawbreakers from anywhere at all. In their hard-hitting, fast-breaking version of justice, the Rangers were quick to lump together all those they thought might be enemies. Consequently, Mexican Texans came to mistrust, if not hate, the same lawmen their Anglo counterparts lauded as heroes.

They showed this distrust in the term they chose for these law enforcers. Among the Mexican people living between the

Nueces River and the Rio Grande, and perhaps elsewhere, the Rangers are called *rinches.* This folk term could be a Hispanic rendering of the word Ranger, as many Anglo-Texans assume, but there is more to it. The mutation of "Ranger" to *rinche* places the term in a category of Spanish words that end in "inche" and are decidedly negative. "Malinche" is the Indian woman who betrayed the Aztecs to the Spanish; *pinche* means small-minded; and *chinche* is a bug or insect.

This negative connotation, this insinuation of meanness and smallness, comes from the history of violence perpetrated by the Rangers against the Mexican community. Their reputation was first established by the fierce fighting and often excessive force used by men known as Texas Rangers during the U.S. war with Mexico in 1846–48 and is perpetuated by reports of Ranger brutality as recently as the 1970s in labor disputes in the Rio Grande Valley. Many Mexican Americans assume that Rangers lump all Hispanics together as criminals or radicals.

Mexican-American literature reveals ample cause for the Hispanic attitude of distrust. Américo Paredes collected a graphic illustration in his research for *With a Pistol in His Hand: A Border Ballad and Its Hero.* The incident occurred in South Texas during the revolutionary year of 1915, when several small groups rose up in armed rebellion against Anglo-Texan authority. Their movement was suppressed by the U.S. army and the Rangers, but Rangers, according to Paredes, did not confine their attacks to the actual rebels. Reprisals extended also to innocent civilians. Mrs. Jo-sefina Flores de Garza of Brownsville in an interview in 1954 gave Paredes insight into how it felt to live through the events of 1915. Then a girl of eighteen and the eldest child of a family that included several younger children, Mrs. Flores de Garza lived near Harlingen on a ranch. When the Rangers arrived to restore order to the area, most of the Mexican-American ranchers moved to town for safety. Her father refused to do so, telling his children "El que nada debe nada teme" (He who is guilty of nothing fears nothing).

When the Rangers arrived at the Flores place, they surrounded the ranch house, then systematically searched all the outbuildings while the family remained indoors. Then the Rangers called for Flores to come outside, and, his daughter said, when he stepped through the door, they shot him without provocation. His two sons ran to his side and were also shot. Then the Rangers came into the Flores house and stole a new pair of chaps before leaving. From other sources Paredes learned that the shock of seeing her father and brothers murdered by the Rangers drove Josefina Flores temporarily insane, and for two days her mother remained inside the ranch house with her terrified children, her deranged daughter, and the corpses of her husband and sons. When a detachment of Regular Army troopers came by on patrol, they buried the bodies of the slain Mexican Americans. Josefina Flores regained her sanity but still became visibly upset when telling of the incident. After forty years she was still afraid of the Rangers and thought they would harm her for telling anyone about the murders.

Some may doubt the objectivity of such a witness or assume that this was an isolated incident. But there is also evidence among Anglo witnesses that Ranger violence was excessive in 1915. Walter Prescott Webb wrote in his history of the Rangers that the situation could be summed up by saying that after the troubles of that year developed, a reign of terror descended upon the Mexican-American population in South Texas. He claimed that in the "orgy of bloodshed" that followed, the Rangers played a prominent role, which many Rangers remembered in shame.

Although such incidents occurred more than half a century ago, many in the Mexican-American community continue to fear the Rangers and look upon them not as heroes but as villains, so much so that a favorite taunt a Mexican-American child might address to a foe is, "*Rinche, pinche, Cara de chinche*" (Mean ranger, face of a bug).

★ José E. Limón, associate professor of anthropology at the University of Texas at Austin, provided this information and recommends that you read Paredes's book for further insights into Mexican-American attitudes toward the Rangers. That's Américo Paredes, "*With a Pistol in His Hand": A Border Ballad and Its Hero* (Austin: University of Texas Press, 1958).

King Cotton and the Iron Horse

Before Texas gold was black, it was white. Cotton ruled the land and the economy of Texas for almost a century, and at the peak of its reign it rode to market on the great iron horse that let farmers push the cotton kingdom steadily westward.

The early Spanish missions in Texas grew cotton for their own use, but not until colonists arrived from the American South did cotton become a cash crop. After winning independence from Mexico, the republic's leaders cited the potential contribution of Texas cotton to the U.S. economy as one of the reasons the United States should annex Texas. By the 1850s, cotton production in the Lone Star state reached the level of other southern states.

On the eve of the Civil War, the bulk of Texas' cotton crop—nearly half a million bales in 1859–60—moved by wagons, flatboats, or small steamboats to Galveston, New Orleans, or some other coastal point for shipment to eastern and European mills. Only a small part of the crop moved over the five hundred miles of rail that had been laid.

Cotton production slowed considerably during the Civil War, but the remarkable technological developments in communication, transportation, and equipment set in motion before the war accelerated after 1870, radically altering the national and international commodities market. In Texas the changes revolutionized the state's

The development of railroads and cotton production complemented one another in the late nineteenth century. This Southern Pacific railyard in Houston was an important regional transportation hub for baled cotton. Courtesy of the Houston Metropolitan Research Center, Houston Public Library.

economic mainstay, the cotton trade. Freight lines offering rapid transport and easy links, commercial cotton gins, and powerful cotton compresses made the staple of the cotton-growing South increasingly available to eastern markets. Fast steamships internationalized the trade. At the same time, a large migration of people into Texas expanded the cotton culture to the west.

The 1870s witnessed a rush in railroad building in Texas—nearly two thousand miles of track were laid in that decade. The Houston and Texas Central Railroad traversed the rich Texas blacklands from Buffalo Bayou to the Red River, where in 1873 it joined with the Missouri, Kansas, and Texas Railroad to link the Lone Star state with the Midwest. The next year Saint Louis investors established a rail connection with Texarkana and then, via the Texas and Pacific, with Dallas. In the following decade various companies built more than six thousand miles of rail in Texas, until the lines stretched from the Sabine River to El Paso and from the Panhandle to the Rio Grande.

Initially the postwar railroad development resulted in a large overland movement of cotton to eastern markets, diverting the trade from Galveston and other Gulf ports. But that trend was reversed, and by 1900 most of the 3.5 million–bale Texas cotton crop left from Galveston, then the largest cotton shipping point in the world. The building of the six-mile twin jetties from the island out into the Gulf of Mexico made Galveston a deep-water port and enabled the harbor to accommodate the largest steamers. The Texas crop that year, valued at over $177 million, represented one-fourth of the total American cotton production.

With the railroads came new settlers. Mostly farmers, these people pushed the frontier ever westward. Where Indians had once hunted buffalo, farmers now grew cotton. By 1900 cotton had reached the High Plains. Railroad development and the expansion of cotton culture encouraged the building of new towns and the opening of new cotton markets. In 1860 the population of Texas had stood at only six hundred thousand people, but at the turn of the century, more than five times that number called themselves Texans.

Expansion of cotton production, railroad development, and the growth of population continued well into the twentieth century. Acreage topped out in the mid-1920s, when over 18 million acres were planted. And railroad trackage peaked in 1932, at seventeen thousand miles. For more than a century King Cotton reigned over Texas. Year after year farmers plowed, planted seed, and hoed the young crop. Year after year they carried the white, fleecy fiber they harvested to the gin and sold the bales. The production, ginning, compressing, warehousing, financing, marketing, and transporting of the staple made cotton the hub of Texas' wheel of commerce. In 1900 the king still sat securely on its Texas throne. A half-century later, wars, depression, and changing times had dethroned the monarch. A new Texas had emerged.

☆ The story of Texas cotton and railroads comes from L. Tuffly Ellis, associate professor of history at the University of Texas at Austin and former director of the Texas State Historical Association. You can read about another aspect of the state's economy during this period in *Sawdust Empire: The Texas Lumber Industry, 1830–1940* by Robert S. Maxwell and Robert D. Baker (College Station: Texas A&M University Press, 1983).

The King Ranch

"Just like a sleeping Giant, sprawling in the sun"—this line from the title song of the 1950s motion picture *Giant* could easily describe the real giant of Texas ranching, the King Ranch. Indeed, this historic ranch does sprawl—across 825,000 acres distributed into four divisions (the original Santa Gertrudis, the Laureles, the Encino, and the Norias) all located along a hundred-mile stretch of South Texas. Although this

This 1940s image of King Ranch cattle shows drivers in the rear, riding "drag" and hurrying the stragglers, while the "swing men" covered the herd's flanks and the "point man" rode in front, avoiding the dust. Courtesy of the Toni Frissell Collection, Library of Congress.

is down from its earlier 1.2 million acres (8 million worldwide in the 1950s), the ranch still covers an area larger than the state of Rhode Island.

When Richard King bought his first 15,500 acres, the Santa Gertrudis Spanish land grant, in 1852, he paid only $300 for it. A mere two years later he spent forty times that in improvements to his ranch.

"Improvement" has been the stock-in-trade of the ranch ever since. Selective breeding of English shorthorn cattle with Brahmans produced the Santa Gertrudis strain, the first new breed ever developed in America, now grown and marketed worldwide. The ranch was also in the forefront of development of the quarter horse, and in 1941 the American Quarter Horse Association awarded its first registration number to Wimpy, a King Ranch stallion that won the grand championship of the Southwestern Exposition and Livestock Show. The King Ranch pioneered the use of dipping vats for tick eradication and introduced cattle prods.

There was a lot to improve on in the beginning. Richard King, born in New York in 1824, had come to Texas in 1846 at the invitation of friend and mentor Mifflin Kenedy to pilot steamboats on the Rio Grande. The land he bought beginning in 1852 — three hundred dollars for the first spread — was rugged and dry; his friends called it King's Folly. Cow camps were raided first by Indians, later by armed bandits and Mexican guerrillas. For two decades King fought them off.

The year 1854 was an important one for the King Ranch, for it saw the ranch's two families begun. King married Henrietta Chamberlain, daughter of a Presbyterian missionary, who would bear his five children and help found a dynasty now in its fifth generation. That year he also crossed the border into Mexico and brought back with him an entire village to work his ranch. These people and their descendants, known as Kineños, or King's Ranch men, brought an almost feudal loyalty to the ranch along with the ranching methods that had developed over time in Mexico from Spanish practices adapted to the region. Kineño loyalty to the Klebergs was sealed by the care provided for them — good pay, housing, schools for their children — and enhanced by the Kleberg family's practice of working side by side with the ranch laborers, often seven days a week.

The Kineños, with their skills and their intergenerational attachment to the land and the *patrón,* are the larger family that make the King Ranch work.

The smaller family, now numbering over sixty, have also maintained a fierce loyalty and sense of responsibility that have held the land together and held the people on it. Ranch management has fallen largely on the shoulders of Klebergs, descended from Richard and Henrietta King through their youngest child, Alice, and her husband, Robert Justus Kleberg. King had first hired Kleberg after the younger man, a lawyer, had beat him and his team of attorneys in a lawsuit. After King's death, his son-in-law took over the ranch's management, although the dominance of Henrietta King's character and interest led neighbors to call the place "the widow's ranch." He developed artesian wells to lure the railroad, enlarged the ranch's holdings, and established family economic dominance in the new town of Kingsville.

In 1925, upon Henrietta King's death and following a disabling illness of his father, Robert Kleberg, Jr., took over the ranch and held it together in the face of court battles among his grandparents' heirs, changing times, and the Great Depression. An inventive genius raised among Kineños who taught him the ways of nature and the ways of cattle, Bob Kleberg persuaded Humble Oil to finance the ranch's depression debt in exchange for leases. Humble began drilling in 1939, and by 1953, 650 wells were producing on ranch land. Bob Kleberg did not rely on oil alone to sustain the ranch, though; he invented a root plow to clear stubborn mesquite,

German immigrants built fine rock fences in Texas. This fine wall surrounds the cemetery at Bethlehem Lutheran Church in Round Top. Photograph by Jack Lewis, courtesy of *Texas Highways* magazine.

The Kentucky Volunteers carried this flag at the Battle of San Jacinto. Now it hangs in the Texas House of Representatives. Photograph by Greg White, courtesy of *Texas Highways* magazine.

◀ *The Spaniards brought missions and forts alike to Texas. This is San Elizario, at El Paso, which began as a chapel at a military post.* Photograph by J. Griffis Smith, courtesy of *Texas Highways* magazine.

First there was the land, then came wave after wave of immigrants—from the Indians, to the Germans who built this neat rock house, to the Vietnamese and Central Americans of recent years.

This view shows Enchanted Rock, just north of Fredericksburg. Photograph by Jack Lewis, courtesy of *Texas Highways* magazine.

Texas has developed much more support for artists since the days of sculptor Elisabet Ney. This piece is "Poetess" by Charles Umlauf of Austin, one of several sculptures that grace the grounds of Laguna Gloria Art Museum in Austin. Photograph by Greg White, courtesy of *Texas Highways* magazine.

Many Texas public buildings of the mid-nineteenth century featured the classical lines of ancient Greece. The Governor's Mansion was begun in 1854. Photograph by Jack Lewis, courtesy of Texas Highways magazine.

Modern cowboys sample old-fashioned "chuck" on a roundup at the Pitchfork Ranch near Guthrie.
Photograph by Jack Lewis, courtesy of *Texas Highways* magazine.

developed forage grasses suited to the South Texas ranges, and expanded ranch holdings to land in Australia, Argentina, Cuba, and elsewhere. He diversified the family's property to include East Texas timberlands. He it was who developed the Santa Gertrudis breed and the King Ranch quarter horse.

When Bob Kleberg died in 1974, an era died. But the King Ranch did not. The modern ranch is vastly different from that of Richard King's time, but four elements of tradition tie the past to the present. Spanish remains the working language of the ranch, although computer languages may dominate the office. The ranch maintains strong ties with and depends on the work of the ranch's people, many of whom are descendants of the original Kineños. The ranch still produces cattle on the same land acquired by King. And the King Ranch is still owned, operated, and fiercely loved by one family, a family that for almost a century and a half has worked hard for the ranch, each other, and the land they love.

☆ David Murrah, director of the Southwest Collection at Texas Tech University, provided information on the King Ranch. If you want to know more about it, read Tom Lea's classic *The King Ranch* (El Paso: Carl Hertzog, 1957) or, for an update on more recent developments, the lengthy article by William Broyles, Jr., "The Last Empire," which appeared in *Texas Monthly* in October, 1980.

Elisabet Ney and Texas Arts

The frontier of settlement rarely coincides with the frontier of the arts. Where life itself is uncertain and unsettled, what art is produced tends to look for certainties rather than to explore artistic horizons. By the end of the nineteenth century, some towns in Texas were becoming mature enough to foster a new artistic sensitivity and to host a few legitimate artists. When in 1892 German sculptor Elisabet Ney moved into the studio she had built on the outskirts of Austin, it marked "a new era in the development of the state," according to biographer Bride Taylor. The new era would see Texas emerge from a cultural frontier with little need or appreciation for the visual arts into a society increasingly aware of painting and sculpture and their importance to the community. The transformation would not be without costs to the artists, and Ney's life illustrates many of the problems and concerns Texas' first professional artists faced.

When Ney opened her Austin studio, only a handful of professional artists made their home in Texas, but by the time she died in 1907 a number of prominent painters and sculptors lived and worked in the state, several cities had the beginnings of museums, and public places as well as private homes displayed the work of artists who considered themselves Texans. Elisabet Ney was hardly the sole, or even the main, cause of this blossoming of activity, yet her contribution was significant. Her work helped nurture an interest in public art and helped raise the artistic merit of other artists' efforts.

Like a number of other early artists in the state—Richard Petri, Hermann Lungkwitz, and Theodore Gentilz, for example—Elisabet Ney was European by birth and training. Born in Munster, Westphalia, on January 26, 1833, into the family of a prosperous stone carver, Ney decided at a young age that she wished to be a sculptor. At nineteen, she became one of the first women to enroll in the Munich Academy of Art. After two years she moved to Berlin, where she studied with distinguished sculptor Christian Daniel Rauch. In combining a neoclassic approach to form, scale, and material with naturalistic detail, her sculpture clearly shows the effect of her mentor's training. In the years after she completed her training she did works for many of the political leaders of the era. Among those whose portraits she modeled are the philologist and collector of fairy tales Jacob Grimm; the Italian revolutionary Giuseppi Garibaldi; the Iron Chancellor of Prussia, Otto von Bismarck; and the "Mad King" of Bavaria, Ludwig II.

No one knows exactly why Ney left Europe in 1870. Perhaps she was involved in political intrigue surrounding Bismarck's attempts to unify Germany under Prussian domination and had to flee. Perhaps, influenced by utopian thinking, she wanted to try a new and simpler life-style. In any

One of the first professional artists in the young state of Texas, Elisabet Ney created sculptures of Stephen F. Austin and Sam Houston, which may be seen in the State Capitol in Austin and at Statuary Hall in Washington, D.C. This 1895 photograph was taken during one of her last visits to her native Germany. Courtesy of the Elisabet Ney Museum, Austin.

event, she moved to Georgia. Then in 1873 she and her husband, a physician named Edmund Montgomery, purchased Liendo Plantation near Hempstead, Texas. For the next decade Ney lay aside her career and devoted her time to running the plantation and raising her son.

When Ney resumed her work in the 1880s, she did not find a promising market for a professional sculptor in Texas. What commissions did exist usually were filled by stonemasons in the larger cities, who could provide polished marble and granite pre-cast figures to serve a number of purposes, including the minimal carving needed for gravestones and small monuments. Ney's first commission finally came when a group of women decided that Texas should have a building at the World's Columbian Exposition in 1893 and that it should be decorated with portraits of the state's heroes. Through the influence of former Governor Oran Roberts, Ney received the commission to produce two statues, one of Sam Houston and the other of Stephen F. Austin, for the Texas Building at the World's Fair.

That assignment marked the beginning of a prolific, new career for Ney. She built her Austin studio, and after completing the statues of Houston and Austin, she produced numerous portraits of great Texans, including Sul Ross, Francis Lubbock, John Reagan, and Joseph Sayers. She worked with women's organizations such as the Daughters of the Republic of Texas to see that her statues of Austin and Houston were placed in both the state and national capitol buildings, where they remain, and, through the efforts of the United Daughters of the Confederacy, she obtained from the state legislature a commission for a memorial to Albert Sidney Johnston erected over his grave in the State Cemetery. She was unable to find anyone to finance some major public monuments she dreamed of, and her efforts to establish an art department at the University of Texas proved unsuccessful. Nonetheless, her studio was a mecca for that part of the Austin community which enjoyed good art and conversation.

Ney attracted as much attention for her eccentric life-style as for her art. Using her maiden name, wearing unusual artist's attire, and living in a simple, classically inspired studio among ornate Victorian homes, she was a source of gossip for those who were not among her small circle of friends and supporters. The public's misunderstandings caused her great distress. "Except for my few friends," she disgustedly wrote to one of her supporters, "I might have fancied myself to have been drifted among the . . . Bushmen while I was in Austin." Still, she remained committed to Texas and to the development of its cultural institutions. On a return voyage from Europe she wrote, "Though I am truly void of what one would call patriotism . . . the appellation of *Texas* has a charm of a peculiar kind, such as the name of no other part of the wide earth."

Ney died in Austin on June 29, 1907, and was buried at Liendo. Her Austin studio and part of its surrounding grounds were later converted into the Elisabet Ney Museum. A number of Ney's friends and supporters then formed the Texas Fine Arts Association, committed to maintain the museum and to promote the growth of fine arts in the state. The Texas Fine Arts Association and the Elisabet Ney Museum are no longer associated, but, true to their origins, they both are active contributors to the development of the arts in Texas.

⭐ Emily Cutrer, an assistant instructor in the American Studies Program at the University of Texas at Austin, culled this information from her doctoral dissertation on Ney. A visit to the Elisabet Ney Museum in Austin would be an excellent way to learn more about the sculptor, her work, and her times.

Capitol and Courthouses

The frontier was won; the state had survived both civil war and its aftermath; the time for permanence, ceremony, and celebration had arrived. As the 1880s opened, interest grew in building a capitol for the State of Texas that would not only accommodate the growing government but also represent the aspirations of the people it served. When the old capitol burned in 1881, the state legislature received its final impetus to act. In 1882 the assembled legislators voted to raise a magnificent new capitol building.

On May 16, 1888, five years after the cornerstone was laid, the citizens of Texas passed beneath the great triumphal-arch entryway and walked for the first time into the building's vast open rotunda. Like its prototype in Washington, the Texas capitol was dominated by a monumental dome that topped a broad ring of classical columns. The Goddess of Liberty crowned the edifice, and the liberty motif used throughout the building honored the constitution of the government it housed. The capitol acknowledged the ancient tradition of Roman Law, architecturally manifested by the domed Pantheon in Rome. Symbolically, by dominating the city below, the building proclaimed rule by law over the land.

As important as the new capitol was, it was nonetheless the county governments, especially in the nineteenth century, that brought this law to the vast countryside. In everyday life it was county officials—for instance, the county judge, county treasurer, county attorney, and county clerk—who administered the law, collected taxes, issued birth certificates and marriage licenses, and sanctioned and recorded the transfer of property. These transactions were all carried out in the county courthouse, a building to which, at a local level, belonged a symbolic role comparable to that of the capitol. State enabling legislation passed in 1881 allowed counties to levy taxes for courthouse construction. This encouraged a great many counties to erect these structures before the end of the nineteenth century, at about the same time that the new capitol building was rising in Austin. Among them are some of the finest architectural achievements in the state: the Hill County Courthouse in Hillsboro, the Ellis County Courthouse in Waxahachie, the Lavaca County Courthouse in Hallettsville, and the Goliad County Courthouse in Goliad.

Rising majestically in the town squares, these monuments to law and justice clearly marked the geopolitical and commercial

Architect Alfred Giles, a British immigrant, designed many nineteenth-century Texas public build-ings, including El Paso's original county courthouse. Completed in 1886, the structure was topped with mansards and Italianate forms. Courtesy of the Otis A. Aultman Collection, El Paso Public Library.

center of each county, and, within the county seat itself, the center of town life and commerce. Their sheer bulk, towering height, and central location brought a vi-sual and symbolic focus to the carefully platted streets almost as surely as the plat maps and land records preserved in their vaults imposed order on the land. With four facades and entryways, these court-houses opened onto each side of the town square, making them equally accessible to every mercantile and banking establish-ment around them. Thus they boldly pro-claimed the union between commerce and government. Their very form expressed the ideals of good government: yawning entryways were open to all, yet broad staircases elevated government above the people. Tall towers carried vague ecclesi-astical associations of a strong faith in

God and moral virtue as well as memories of the great city halls of the republican city-states of the Renaissance. Constructed of brick and stone, the buildings conveyed a clear sense of permanence, and their monumentality instilled confidence in the institutions they housed.

One hundred years later many of these great temples of justice still stand in the small towns of Texas to remind us of the pride and confidence the citizens of these communities had in their government and of the optimism they held for the future of their state.

☆ The information on these public buildings comes from Kenneth A. Breisch, director of survey and planning for the Texas Historical Commission. If you would like to learn more about these buildings, see Willard B. Robinson's *Texas Public Buildings of the Nineteenth Century* (Austin: University of Texas Press, 1974), which features many fine photographs.

The Cowboy

A cattle boom that lasted only twenty years, peaking in the mid 1880s, launched the American cowboy on a century-long career as a mythical national hero embodying all the American virtues. Ranching and the working cowboy are still very much a part of Western life. The contemporary working cowboy sometimes sees himself — and is seen by others — in the image of the mythical motion-pictures and television cowboy, but the very real skills with which he makes his living are essentially those of his forerunner, the open-range cowboy of the 1870s and 1880s.

That early cowboy drew upon two traditions for his skills and equipment. The Spanish-American cowboy, or vaquero, had been active in northern New Spain, including California and Texas, since the beginning of the eighteenth century. The Anglo-Americans and blacks who came into Texas in the 1820s brought with them a second tradition, that of the cattle herder of the Southern Coastal Plains.

It Texas, the two traditions met and mixed. After the American Civil War an open-range ranching industry developed, first in Texas and then on the ranges to the northwest. There was money in the north now to pay for good food, and the development of railroads and refrigeration made it possible to meet the new demand by shipping beef to the cities in the East. The open-range ranching that resulted was based on the grazing of cattle on unfenced public land and featured semiannual cooperative roundups and long trail drives from the grazing ranges to shipping points. The gear and the skills of both traditions that nourished the cowboy were called into play. The hybrid Texas cowpoke followed this industry and spread his skills, techniques, and dress all over the West.

Overgrazing and a series of disastrous

Dustin Farnum played the leading role in Owen Wister's drama The Virginian *when it opened in New York in 1904. After a few months, the production went on tour, and it continued as a road show for a decade. The script provided material for three movie versions and inspired a television series in the 1950s. Courtesy of the Manuscripts Division, Library of Congress.*

popular imagination. In the 1880s the illustrated press, through magazines such as *Frank Leslie's, Harper's,* and the *Police Gazette,* presented the cowboy to the public in woodcut illustrations as a rough-and-tumble individualist. At the same time, the Buffalo Bill Wild West production brought cowboys in the flesh to the East in an act called "Cowboy Fun" that featured trick riding and trick shooting. In 1886 a thirty-year-old Texas cowboy, Charlie Siringo, published the first cowboy memoir, *A Texas Cow Boy.* By the end of the century, it had been followed by a string of cowboy books—the most popular, Theodore Roosevelt's *Ranch Life and the Hunting Trail* (1888) and Owen Wister's *The Virginian* (1902). Both books portrayed the cowboy as brave, soft-spoken, democratic, and virtuous. Frederic Remington, who became America's best-loved Western painter and illustrator in the early 1900s, illustrated Roosevelt's work.

The development of the cinema at the turn of the century fixed the cowboy forever in America's imagination. Actually, the movies have shown us two cowboys. The flamboyant showman, who stepped out of the Buffalo Bill show onto the screen, was personified by Tom Mix, Gene Autry, and Roy Rogers. The quiet, virtuous man of action, derived from Wister's *Virginian,* was protrayed by William S. Hart, Randolph Scott, Gary Cooper, and John Wayne. In films, and the new medium television, the 1950s cowboy image merged with that of the lawman and avenger; the pistol displaced the guitar, which had displaced the lasso, as the symbol of the mythical cowboy. In the 1960s the cowboy became

winters in the late 1880s destroyed open-range ranching. After 1888 the industry began to reorganize to utilize fenced pastures, improved stock through controlled breeding, winter feed crops, and, eventually, trucks and trailers. But the open-range cowboy had already caught the

a symbol representing first masculinity and, in the 1970s, the leisure associated with the "Southwestern life-style." So potent has the cowboy symbol been that advertisers—from cigarette and beer companies to fast food chains and high-fashion clothiers—have worked him into their presentations.

Whatever the image, though, the reality has been work, and that work, with horses and cattle, riding and roping, still earns the Southwestern cowboy a living.

⭐ These insights into the cowboy mystique were provided by Lonn Taylor, assistant director for public programs at the National Museum of American History, Smithsonian Institution. Charles Siringo's lively memoirs, *A Texas Cowboy,* are available in many reprint editions for those who would like to read a personal account of the early days.

Demon Rum

A vote for this or that candidate was a vote for Demon Rum. For many Texans politics was that simple between 1900 and 1920. Few issues in American history have so clearly defined the vote for so long a time as Prohibition did. Every candidate for a Texas public office had to address that issue first, and a significant number of voters considered no other stands in determining their votes.

The Prohibitionists' crusade sprang, to a large extent, from women's convictions that alcohol threatened the family, which was certainly the very foundation of their personal lives if not of American civic and cultural life. Perhaps women had another, subconscious reason for their dislike of "the accursed bowl." In the nineteenth century drinking was a male privilege, an overt sign of the double standard of morality and behavior. Thus, Prohibition may have offered a socially acceptable way to attack male supremacy.

In any event, the Prohibition movement began in earnest in Texas in 1885, with the organization of the first local chapter of the Women's Christian Temperance Union, and intensified after 1907, when the Anti-Saloon League arrived in Texas. Women did most of the grass-roots work of spreading the Prohibitionist message through speaking, raising money, lecturing, and writing and handing out pamphlets. Women also constituted the majority of the memberships of the temperance societies and of the Protestant churches that gave the movement its revivalist fervor.

The Prohibitionist movement nonetheless also had a firm base of support among men. Many saw "demon rum" as a terrible threat to the nation's moral fiber and to the entire system of traditional values upheld by rural and small-town life; this view was enough to inspire hate. The issue of Prohibition found much of its strength in farming families whose children had left the country and now lived and worked in the vice- and sin-ridden urban centers

Women of varied ages, races, and social classes supported Protestant religious leaders in urging passage of prohibition statutes, as these women in Lufkin demonstrated in 1915. The political skills women acquired in battling legalized drinking proved valuable in their quest to obtain suffrage. Courtesy of the Kurth Memorial Library, Lufkin, Texas.

of Houston, Dallas, and San Antonio. Most supporters of Prohibition in Texas were Anglo fundamentalist Protestants in the farming communities and small towns of North and West Texas.

Two groups led the political campaign against alcohol: the pastors of Baptist and Methodist churches, who often were officers of the Anti-Saloon League, and the Progressives, who were liberal reformers within the Texas Democratic party. Conservative businessmen and many mainstream Democrats resisted what they saw as government interference with individual choices under Prohibition. The Pro-

gressive Democrats saw Prohibition as the way to return morality to public life in Texas. They believed that Prohibition would defeat the last of the powerful corporate special interests in Texas, the brewers and saloon owners, and would blunt the influence of the South Texas county "bosses," whose "political machines" routinely purchased Mexican votes. Prohibition, then, also took on racist tones. Most Mexican and German Texans did not see drinking as a sin, and black Texas voters also tended to oppose Prohibition. Anglo Protestants were determined to prevail, in Texas and elsewhere.

World War I and women's suffrage finally gave Texas Prohibitionists the victory, even if it was to prove temporary. Arguing that Texas must provide wholesome environments for military personnel stationed in the state, the "drys" pushed through a law banning the sale of liquor within ten miles of any training base. At the same time, in the spring of 1918, the legislature ratified the Eighteenth Amendment to the U.S. Constitution and passed a statewide prohibition bill as well.

Throughout the Prohibition struggle, the liquor interests, for obvious reasons, had opposed women's suffrage and contributed the single largest sum of money to the campaign to defeat it. In the 1918 Democratic gubernatorial primary race between the "wet" candidate, James E. "Pa" Ferguson, and the Prohibitionist incumbent, William P. Hobby, the male vote split evenly. But Texas women voted for Hobby by a margin of ten to one, giving him the Democratic nomination by almost 150,000 votes. Similarly, in May, 1920, when the "wets" lost control of the Texas Democratic party, their leader correctly blamed "the women and the preachers." The white ribbon, symbol of the WCTU, had for the moment bound Demon Rum.

☆ Elizabeth Enstam, research associate in the history department of Southern Methodist University, furnished these facts about women and Prohibition in Texas. To learn more about this subject, she recommends that you read the two books from which she drew much of this material: Ruth Bordin, *Women and Temperance: The Quest for Power and Liberty, 1873–1900* (Philadelphia: Temple University Press, 1981); and Lewis L. Gould, *Progressivism and Prohibition* (Austin: University of Texas Press, 1973).

Hogg and Populism

Raise "more hell and less corn" if you want a greater share of the wealth, cried the Kansas Pythoness Mary E. Lease, outspoken advocate of agrarian reform. Lease joined other agrarian leaders, such as "Pitchfork Ben" Tillman and "Sockless Jerry" Simpson, in denouncing businessmen, bankers, and railroad owners as the exploiters of the farmers. They also advocated a more inflationary monetary system, the "free and unlimited coinage of silver," as the ideal panacea for what ailed the nation's farmers. Texans joined with Lease and other leaders in the thrust for agrarian reform, but as usual they wanted to do it their way.

Under the umbrella of the Patrons of Husbandry, or the Grange, farmers exerted significant political influence in Texas as early as the mid-1870s, when they controlled the convention that wrote the state's constitution. Political power at the state level did not necessarily mean economic

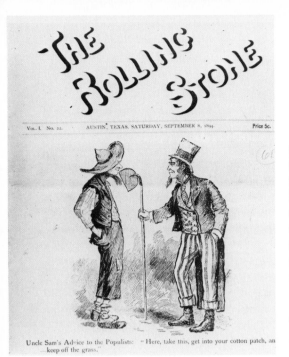

Uncle Sam's Advice to the Populists: "Here, take this, get into your cotton patch, an keep off the grass."

The Rolling Stone, *published in Austin, was one of several Texas populist periodicals of the late nineteenth century. Articles and illustrations frequently held Uncle Sam and northern financial interests responsible for the economic plight of Texas farmers.* Courtesy of the Barker Texas History Center, the University of Texas at Austin.

power, however, because few farmers could agree on a common policy. In the legislature, where they were together, they wielded power; at home, and separated, they were often victims of the stronger forces of nature and of wealthy men.

The Texas agricultural picture had changed dramatically after the American Civil War. Its center shifted to the blacklands of the Central Prairies and on to the High Plains when irrigation made agriculture practical in more arid regions. Cotton had been the dominant crop even before the war, but afterwards it became the cash-crop specialization of every Texas farmer who yearned to earn enough money to improve his lot. In 1870 Texas farmers produced a $10 million cotton crop; thirty

years later the crop was worth ten times that. Texans produced 35,000 bales of cotton in 1870, and more than 2.5 million bales in 1900, but the price per pound dropped from thirty-five cents to five cents or less and overall farm income dropped from $88 million to $68 million per year, meaning that farmers had to produce more each year just to stay even. And natural disasters such as too little or too much rain made the gamble even worse. The result was an increase in the sharecrop, share-tenant, and crop-lien systems in Texas as well as in the remainder of the South.

Most farmers fell into greater debt no matter how hard they worked. They knew no one to blame personally, so they blamed the system, the banks, railroads, and insurance companies, their natural sources of credit, and supported the Farmers' Alliance and Populism in order to have a greater voice in redressing their grievances.

Populism included all sorts of agrarians in Texas. Born from the Texas Alliance, which first appeared in Lampasas in 1875, after a series of false starts it spread across the Cross Timbers area. By August, 1888, it claimed three hundred thousand members. Two of these were Charles W. Macune, who saw the multisectional cooperative movement as a means of achieving Radical economic reform, and William Lamb, who used the movement to launch a third-party political revolt.

Macune had come to Texas from Wisconsin, where he was born in 1851. He settled near Burnet in 1874, where he founded a newspaper and practiced law and medicine. Sometime in the 1880s, he joined the Farmers' Alliance and rose to alliance leadership. Strongly committed to economic cooperation, at Waco in 1887 he proposed the Alliance Exchange and the subtreasury plan. He also backed the unification with the Louisiana Farmers' Alliance and the Arkansas Wheel that occurred in 1887. Macune went on to become the first president of the national Farmers' Alliance and Cooperative Union of America.

Always a centralist, Macune was unhappy with third-party politics. Thus he supported Democrat James Stephen Hogg, a lawyer and district attorney in Smith County. Hogg became attorney general in 1886 and won a reputation as a reformer by supporting the nation's second antitrust law and breaking up the Texas Traffic Association. Unhappy with powerful railroad corporations, in 1890 Hogg successfully ran for governor on the issue of a state railroad regulatory commission. He later alienated many members of the Alliance by making the Railroad Commission appointive and not elective.

Meanwhile, Macune moved to Washington, D.C., in 1889 and founded the *National Economist*. He was a delegate to the Populist convention in Saint Louis, Missouri, in 1892. He continued to oppose political activity by the National Farmers'

Alliance, and in 1893 he resigned as editor of the *National Alliance* and returned to Texas.

In 1892 Hogg won reelection by defeating the Conservative Democrat George Clark and the radical Populist candidate Thomas Nugent. His administration passed the famous "Hogg Laws" and additional ones that reformed the prison system and upgraded public schools and college education. Many consider his administration the best in Texas history, but more radical historians look upon his tenure as that of a progressive who cut the heart out of substantial political reforms by advocating more moderate ones.

The dispute over whether to support Hogg or the Populists destroyed the Farmers' Alliance, which by 1895 had disappeared. Hogg left elective office and made a fortune in law, real estate, and oil, but his position as the symbol of Texas reform remains unrivaled.

☆ Robert A. Calvert, associate professor of history at Texas A&M University, provided this information on Texas progressivism. You can find out more about this era in Texas history from Alwyn C. Barr's book *From Reconstruction to Reform* (Austin: University of Texas Press, 1971).

Women on the Urban Frontier

Frontier women lacked many of the conveniences of their sisters back East. But

what they lacked in convenience, they often made up for in opportunity. Even on

Josephine Theis (back left) worked for an Austin retailer for a year, then opened her own millinery shop a few blocks north of her former employer on Congress Avenue. She become a major Austin retailer of hats and antiques during the first half of the twentieth century. Courtesy of the Austin History Center, Austin Public Library (PICA 15505).

rural homesteads, farms, and ranches, the life of women was in some ways more nearly equal with their husbands' than in less demanding circumstances. Wives' primary roles were as homemakers, but many were also partners with their husbands in extracting the family livelihood from the raw country. And the towns of frontier Texas between 1840 and 1900 provided women opportunities perhaps available nowhere else in the West.

Towns gave women the chance to turn their homemaking skills into cash. Women on the urban frontier of Texas ran schools and taught music lessons in their homes. Those who were especially skilled at needlework owned and ran dressmaking and millinery shops, often in partnership with other women. With frontier towns expanding so quickly, women with extra rooms in their homes could open boardinghouses and benefit financially from the newcomers' need for meals and lodging. Some women ran restaurants, confectioneries, laundries, and bakeries. Of course, even on the frontier, opportunity was not equal. Women who had few special skills, who were recent immigrants to the United

States, or who were black, found fewer openings; they usually worked as laundresses or as domestic servants.

On their own, women who worked usually did so in areas that utilized their homemaking skills, but as partners with their husbands, many women found other careers in family businesses. The earliest city directories often listed both husband and wife as owners of businesses. Family records show that sometimes it was the wife who kept the accounts, handled the correspondence, and managed the money, while her husband traveled to find new customers, make deliveries, or seek new opportunities for expanding the business. In this way frontier women in Texas began to run dry goods stores and hotels, to edit and write for newspapers, and even to operate livery and sale stables. If they were widowed, these women were experienced and able to take over the family business, often rearing young children at the same time. In all, some 15 to 25 percent of the adult female population of the urban frontier in Texas found employment outside the home. Thus, the young towns of Texas offered women much the same thing they offered men: opportunity.

When the railroads reached a frontier town, the "boom" they brought created still more jobs for women. The demand increased for schools, boardinghouses, dressmaking and millinery, and domestic service, among other things. Larger hotels needed chambermaids, and the increased number of restaurants and cafes required waitresses and cooks. As business expanded for dry goods stores, their owners sought women to assist customers with sales.

Out-of-state companies needed women agents to sell sewing machines, notions, or patent medicines to other women, often door-to-door. With the railroads also came the telegraph, and often young women worked as the telegraphers. By 1880 post offices hired women as stamp, register, and copying clerks. Women ran newsstands and sold cigars and candies from booths in hotel lobbies. Industry followed the railroads, and, as elsewhere, women found jobs in cigar, paper and box, textile, clothing, and cracker factories.

By the late 1880s a few women in the larger towns were entering the medical profession, most as nurses, but a few as physicians. By the early 1900s a few women pharmacists, bacteriologists, dentists, opticians, and pathologists appeared in city directories. Women entered the legal profession far more slowly than the medical fields.

In the early twentieth century large numbers of Texas women secured employment as telephone operators, stenographers, or clerks in offices. In later decades these positions came to be stereotyped as "woman's work," so fully did women dominate them. In some ways, the appearance of significant numbers of these "women's" jobs was itself a sign of the passing of the frontier.

☆ This information on women's economic role in Texas frontier towns comes from Elizabeth Enstam, history research associate at Southern Methodist University. Diverse views of Texas through women's eyes are presented in Jo Ella Powell Exley, ed., *Texas Tears and Texas Sunshine: Voices of Frontier Women* (College Station: Texas A&M University Press, 1985).

The stream of foreign immigrants into Texas continued in the twentieth century. The Jewish Immigrants' Information Bureau assisted these European arrivals entering the country at Galveston's port in 1907. Courtesy of the Archives of Temple B'nai Israel, Galveston.

European Immigrants

Texas has nearly always been ethnically diverse, but until recently, few stopped to think about it. They just accepted the fact that one neighbor was German and another Norwegian and thought of them as fellow Americans and fellow Texans. If they were white and the neighbor black, or if they were Anglo and the neighbor Hispanic, the relationship might or might not be as pleasant. Everyone knew there were differences, but these differences received little attention from Texans until the present century.

By the time Spanish rule over Texas ended, there were already more Anglos than Spaniards or Mexicans who lived here, perhaps as many as ten times more. They came mostly from the southern states of the American Union and, extending the culture of the Deep South, occupied the

99

territory as far west as San Antonio and Goliad, which brought them into contact with Hispanic and Irish settlements. Only the remnants of Spanish settlements at El Paso and Santa Fe were of any consequence beyond the Anglo frontier.

Yet there were always pockets of difference. After the mid-1840s Germans immigrated to Central Texas in significant numbers. Henri Castro's Alsatians and Johan Rierson's Norwegians also made inroads during the same decade. These arrivals, like the Anglos already in Texas, were mostly North European in heritage.

Immigration patterns began to change later in the century, under the influence of political and economic forces in Europe. Immigrants, some of whom eventually found their way to Texas, continued to arrive in the United States from England, Germany, and Holland, but more and more people left homes in southern and central Europe for the promise of America. Czechs, Poles, Italians, Slavs, Greeks, and Jews from all nations came to the United States for new starts.

This shift in cultural, or ethnic, groups had a pronounced influence on the strength of Western versus Eastern European influence in the United States and in Texas. The last decade of the nineteenth century was the first in which less than 50 percent of Europe's emigrants came from its western countries. Within two decades the figure dropped to 17 percent. This shift not only accounts for much of the ethnic prejudice in the United States, it also defines the later immigration patterns for Texas.

The coming of the railroad made it easier for immigrants to move west, and, partly because Texas had more railroad miles than any other state of the Union by 1900, it received a significant share of the new immigrants. Many, particularly Jews from eastern Europe, entered through such ports as Galveston. The Texas population increased from near 1 million to more than 3 million persons between 1870 and 1900. These newcomers helped fill in the western Panhandle and Trans-Pecos regions, while newer groups from everywhere, including China and Japan, swelled urban centers. And it had only begun. Immigration to Texas in the twentieth century would assume even more dramatic forms.

☆ Information on European immigrants in Texas in the nineteenth century was provided by John Davis, former director of research at the Institute of Texan Cultures. The Institute has published an impressive series of pamphlets and books on Texas ethnic groups that could help you learn more about the various peoples who have become Texans.

The Great Galveston Hurricane

"Child, I can't tell you how that water came. It just come pouring in. There wasn't nothing to stop it. We went on upstairs because the water came in downstairs. I was

Debris at Broadway and 14th Street testified to the destructive power of the storm that lashed Galveston in 1900. Though Sacred Heart Catholic Church received severe damage, the nearby Bishop's Palace (center background) *was spared.* Courtesy of the Rosenberg Library and Texas History Center, Galveston.

praying to the Lord and I never thought about anything else." Ella Belle Ramsey remembered vividly the hurricane that hit Galveston in September of 1900. It was the greatest natural disaster in U.S. history.

Although eleven hurricanes had struck the Texas coast in the nineteenth century and one had destroyed nearby Indianola only four years earlier, Galveston was unprepared for the storm of 1900. The people had done little for protection; worse, they had taken sand from the dunes, eliminating a natural breakwater. They enjoyed a false security, convinced that the ocean's devastating waves could not reach them because of sandbars and shallow water and that the bay behind them would absorb the shock of any storm.

In early September, 1900, the U.S. Weather Service warned its local climatologist, Isaac M. Cline, about an approaching hurricane. He, in turn, notified residents within three blocks of the beach to seek higher ground, so Galvestonians were not surprised by the hurricane's arrival. They were amazed, though, at its severity.

The hurricane swerved inland over Galveston on September 8, quickly covering the island with water. It totally destroyed the first six blocks of houses along the shore of the Gulf of Mexico—an estimated thirty-six hundred houses—caused $30 million in damages, and killed an estimated ten thousand—six thousand people on the island and another four thousand on the mainland. Many of the homes had been built on stilts to raise them above floods, but the storm battered them with floating debris and winds that reached an estimated 120 miles per hour. The wind velocity could only be an estimate because the weather station anemometer itself blew away; before it did, it had registered 84 miles per hour. The storm surge reached 15.7 feet, almost doubling the previous high-water mark of 8.2 feet.

When it was over, the stunned survivors staggered out into a calm, sunlit Sunday morning to find their city in ruins. "Dreadful sights met our gaze on all sides," said Joseph Cline, the brother of the climatologist. A thirty-block-long line of debris, head high and four- to ten-feet deep, was filled with the broken remnants of urban life. Anything located less than eight feet above the level of the first floor was damaged by salt water. The British ship *Roma* took out three of the four bridges to the mainland when the hurricane pushed it sideways down the channel of the harbor. Worst of all were the bodies of human beings and animals that shortly began to decay in the warm, moist air.

Some talked of abandoning the town, but the majority of people remained and rebuilt. Workmen cremated bodies on

burning piles of debris, restored urban facilities, and cleaned the townsite. Exaggerated news accounts reported rampant looting and widespread hysteria, but in fact there was little of either. Cooperation among the survivors remained high, the "Galveston Spirit." After the cleanup was completed, the town began a decade of preparation for future storms. A seventeen-foot-high concrete seawall was built, the grade level of the city was raised, and an all-weather causeway was constructed. In the process, Galvestonians invented and popularized the commission form of city government. Their defenses against nature worked well: in a comparable storm in 1915 only eight people died.

While Galveston used its energy and resources for protection, its rival, Houston, was building a ship channel through Buffalo Bayou into Galveston Bay on the Gulf. Houston was already a railroad center, and now it was able to offer deepwater port facilities with a twenty-five-mile-long watercourse for the location of manufacturers. These installations were in place in time to take advantage of the petroleum boom of the twentieth century. By 1930 Houston had outdistanced Galveston and was on its way to becoming an energy capital. Galveston, in contrast, had experienced stagnation and the fate of becoming a pleasant middle-sized vacation town still periodically visited by Gulf hurricanes.

☆ The events of the 1900 Galveston hurricane were recounted by David McComb, professor of history at Colorado State University. If you would like to read an account of the storm based on the memories of its survivors, see John Edward Weems, *A Weekend in September* (1957; College Station: Texas A&M University Press, 1980).

Texas Entrepreneurs

"I thank the Ku Klux Klan for my success. If it hadn't been for their cross-burnings there, I would have died a well-to-do small town jeweler. But they forced me out of town and now look at what I've become." What Morris Zale had become was one of the wealthiest men in a state noted for citizens who amassed great fortunes.

Texans have shown a trial-and-error quality as workbench inventors and entrepreneurs almost since serious colonization began in the 1820s. Samuel May Williams, secretary to empresario Stephen F. Austin, joined with Thomas F. McKinney, a farmer-rancher, when Texas was still a Mexican colony to establish a mercantile firm that grew until its credit rating was superior to that of the Republic of Texas. These partners furnished about a quarter of the funds used to fight Texas' revolutionary war aginst Mexico and convinced U.S. merchants, uncertain about the infant Republic's ability to meet its obligations, that if Texas could not pay, they would stand good for the bills. The American merchants trusted McKinney and Williams, and the Republic of Texas received the supplies it needed to obtain its independence.

Not long after that, a farmer-rancher who doubled as a surveyor and newspaper publisher and helped to develop Galveston Island started tinkering with food condensation. He amassed a hundred-thousand-dollar fortune, a considerable sum in those days, by the time he was fifty years old, but he lost it all pushing a product he called a meat biscuit, a sort of de-hydrated Spam. He thought the product would prove a boon to sailors and overland travelers trekking across the unsettled deserts to the goldfields of California. In the mid-1850s this entrepreneur lived in New York City, vainly trying to market his product and living on thirty dollars a month. His wife had left him because of his fall from affluence, and his children were scattered.

Then Gail Borden conceived the idea of condensing milk for convenience and safekeeping. With only a year and a half of formal schooling and no laboratory training, he attacked the problem the only way a pioneer knew how to proceed: by persevering in trial and error.

When the American Civil War began, Borden, broke and pressed by debts falling due with frightening regularity, was rescued by, for him, a fortuitous circumstance. The war was fought in the hot South, where milk was difficult to obtain and could not be kept for any length of time without spoiling. The Union army tried his product and, deciding it would provide adequate milk for soldiers' coffee, bought it in wholesale quantities. By the end of the war Borden owned processing plants in Illinois and New York and had other plants under his license throughout the North. He returned to Texas to live out the remainder of his life. Texas' first notable philanthropist, he underwrote schools and churches for both whites and freed blacks. When he died in 1874 at Columbus, Texas, his descendants shared an income of a hundred thousand dollars a year from his holdings. The company that he founded, the Borden Company, remains a billion-dollar enterprise listed in *Fortune Magazine*'s top five hundred corporations.

Another, later Texas immigrant who exemplified the bootstrap story typical of entrepreneurs was Morris B. Zale. Zale was born along the Russian-Polish border at the beginning of the twentieth century. Because Jews were being persecuted in Russia, his family emigrated to Texas, where Zale began work in a Fort Worth jewelry store owned by an uncle while he attended Central High School. Zale later quit his job as a clerk to form his own small enterprise in the back of a drug store on the square at Graham, about a hundred miles northwest of Fort Worth. He prospered there through hard work, but his prospects were probably limited in the small town. Then he was run out of town during the resurgence of Ku Klux Klan activity following World War I.

Zale moved to Wichita Falls, then in the midst of an oil boom, where he worked for another uncle. Almost overnight the town jumped from a sleepy Red River Val-

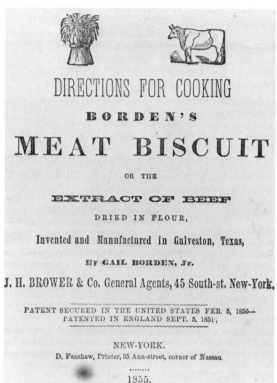

DIRECTIONS FOR COOKING

BORDEN'S

MEAT BISCUIT

OR THE

EXTRACT OF BEEF

DRIED IN FLOUR,

Invented and Manufactured in Galveston, Texas,

BY GAIL BORDEN, Jr.

J. H. BROWER & Co. General Agents, 45 South-st. New-York.

PATENT SECURED IN THE UNITED STATES FEB. 5, 1850—
PATENTED IN ENGLAND SEPT. 5, 1851,

NEW-YORK.
D. Fanshaw, Printer, 35 Ann-street, corner of Nassau.
....
1855.

Gail Borden's invention of a meat biscuit did not catch on, but he continued with experiments and his later process for condensed milk proved valuable. The Union army bought the milk in quantity, launching a successful American corporation. Courtesy of D. Fanshaw and the University of Texas Institute of Texan Cultures, San Antonio.

ley community into a brawling, bustling city of forty thousand people with a great deal of money to spend. Zale observed that the jewelry stores in Wichita Falls were doing a thriving business in what he called the suddenly rich "carriage trade." With true business acumen, he reasoned

Morris Zale opened his first jewelry store in 1924 at 8th and Ohio streets in Wichita Falls, Texas. His desire to employ numerous relatives contributed to his establishment of a chain of jewelry stores later. Courtesy of Zale Corporation, Irving, Texas.

that people of more modest means probably liked jewelry equally well but could not afford items of such quality. So he left his salaried position to move down the street and open a store he called Zale's. He sent the word around that he was ready to do business on a "dollar down, dollar a week" basis. His was the first credit retail jewelry store in Texas, possibly the first in the nation, and it opened up the jewelry trade to an entirely new class of consumers, who did not have much money individually but collectively represented significant purchasing power. Zale went on to purchase a near-bankrupt store in Tulsa, then one in Oklahoma City, and another in Amarillo.

Because of its superior transportation facilities, Zale later moved his headquarters to Dallas, where it became the control center for more than sixteen hundred retail outlets throughout the nation plus another six hundred high-quality stores operating under their original names. His firm owned factories in Israel, the Netherlands, Brazil, and Japan; shoe stores; clothing stores; sporting goods outlets; and still other enterprises. Zale's is in the billion-dollar earnings category but remains a family-operated business that somehow has managed to maintain a personal touch among its thousands of employees.

Both of these stories, the nineteenth-century saga of Borden and the twentieth-century success story of Zale, feature the Texas entrepreneur, a person willing to risk a secure living for the bigger opportunity, to grow through providing a service, to gamble intelligently, and to come out on top.

☆ Information on these two celebrated Texas entrepreneurs was provided by Joe B. Frantz, professor of history at Corpus Christi State University and professor emeritus at the University of Texas at Austin. His book *Gail Borden, Dairyman to a Nation* (Norman: University of Oklahoma Press, 1951) tells the story of that fascinating man.

Spindletop

"Now that we have got her, boys, how are we going to close her up?" The geyser at Spindletop, which none of the major oil companies had been willing to take a chance on, flowed so freely that its drillers almost at once had to start looking for ways to control it. In only nine days the discovery well produced 800,000 barrels of oil. Surrounding rice fields were covered, the grass was soaked with oil, and the danger of fire loomed big. At last, on the gusher's tenth day, the well was capped, and a valve began to regulate the flow of Texas oil. But nearby Beaumont and Texas itself were already indelibly marked by the black liquid.

Decades before the Spindletop discovery, oil had been found near Nacogdoches and San Antonio. It had been produced in commercial quantities near Corsicana, where the Texas oil industry was really born. Two things made Spindletop different and gave it a significance far beyond that of earlier Texas wells: the quantity of oil found was prodigious, and the geological formation from which the oil was produced extended over much of the Gulf Coast.

The ambitions of Patillo Higgins, an almost stereotypical Irish-American dreamer, gave birth to the Spindletop discovery. Higgins had been, at various times, a log-

Spindletop's Boiler Avenue reflected the dense growth of the Texas oil industry following a discovery of petroleum at the salt dome near Beaumont in 1901. Courtesy of the American Petroleum Institute, Washington, D.C.

ger, a real estate speculator, a mechanic, and a draftsman and had once tried to promote a brick factory to serve the growing coastal area market. In 1892 he organized the Gladys City Oil, Gas and Manufacturing Company to drill a wildcat well on a hill south of Beaumont. After leasing or purchasing nearly four thousand acres of land, he ran out of funds, and his project was taken over by Anthony F. Lucas, an Austrian engineer and former naval officer.

Lucas tried to interest Standard Oil Company of New Jersey in the project in order to raise additional funds. Standard

Oil was intrigued and investigated the investment thoroughly, but its executives concluded that commercial quantities of oil were not likely to be found. The project might have lapsed then had not two eastern wildcatters taken an interest in the idea of Higgins and Lucas. James M. Guffey and Thomas M. Galey were so convinced of the potential that they invested money they had made in Pennsylvania and West Virginia oil fields into the risky hunt for Texas oil. They hired Al and Jim Hammill, two drillers from Corsicana, to drill the wildcat well, using a rotary drilling rig not yet standard in either Texas or the rest of the country.

The Hammill brothers undertook the job for two dollars a foot, cheap pay for the work it turned out to require. It took them two weeks to drill through 285 feet of sand and gravel. Then they hit a gas pocket and finally struck hard rock at 880 feet. The work was risky because they never knew what formation and hazards they might encounter next.

Patillo Higgins's dreams, Anthony Lucas's speculations, the investments of Guffey and Galey, and the work of the Hammill brothers and their crew finally paid off during the first month of the twentieth century. At 10:30 in the morning on January 10, 1901, as the well reached 1,020 feet, oil suddenly gushed over the top of the wooden rig and up into the air. For several days no one knew how much oil the new well would produce. Captain Lucas, more a scientist than a promoter, estimated it flowed at a few thousand barrels a day. It actually must have produced at almost 100,000 barrels of oil per day. Additional drilling on the salt-dome structure showed clearly that Spindletop was capable of producing as much oil as the entire state of Pennsylvania. Texas had not just a new oil field, but a field so vast that it would precipitate the restructuring of the oil industry in the United States.

The famous Standard Oil Trust, under legal attack in several states, could no longer monopolize the development of oil once the Spindletop well was completed. There was too much of it, and it was too far from Standard's other large operations. There were new competitors, too. Within

six months the predecessors of the Gulf Oil Corporation and the Texas Company were organized to produce and refine Spindletop oil. Just as important, Texans were already on the scene, and from the beginning they played a large role in the development of the petroleum industry in their state.

Governor James Stephen Hogg, who already had tangled with the Standard Trust during his tenure as attorney general, was one of the new oilmen. So were Robert Lee Blaffer and William P. Farish, two of the founders of that Texas giant, the Humble Oil and Refining Company. The Moonshine Oil Company was formed by Walter Sharp, Ed Prather, and Howard Hughes, each of whom later built his own oil operation and major manufacturing company related to the oil industry, and who presaged both the image and the reality of the daring, successful, and, consequently, wealthy independent Texas oilman. All of the oilmen from Higgins and Lucas to Blaffer and Hughes provided the real stuff from which the Texas myth of the oilman was later generated. After Spindletop, Texas grit had a lot of oil in it.

The importance of Spindletop can hardly be overstated. Oil allowed the state's economy to diversify; until then it had been based narrowly on agribusiness, except in East Texas, where the timber industry still provided jobs and dollars. The subsequent discovery of oil on school and university lands poured billions of dollars into the state's public education system. Jobs in exploration and production, in refining and marketing, and in related manufacturing industries have fed hundreds of thousands of families in Texas. The money and the skill associated with the oil industry have contributed greatly to the emergence of the modern economy and society of Texas.

☆ Roger M. Olien, professor of history at the University of Texas, Permian Basin, provided this information on Spindletop. To find out more about the history of Texas oil, see *Early Texas Oil: A Photographic History, 1866–1936* by Walter Rundell, Jr. (College Station: Texas A&M University Press, 1977).

Neighbor in Revolution

Texas might have declared political independence from Mexico in 1836, but a shared border and a common heritage assured that Texas and Mexico would continue to affect each other's destinies. Nowhere has that reciprocal influence been clearer than in Mexico's twentieth-century revolutions.

Most of the Mexican revolutionary movements in the first two decades of this century started in Texas; none could have succeeded had it not been for the men and war supplies that crossed the Rio Grande from Texas. Moreover, the fervor of Mexican border towns during the upheaval spilled over into their American sister cities. Men were recruited in Texas, and although American troops tried to stop the flow of arms and ammunition, weapons crossed Texas border points destined for rebel factions in Mexico. Refugees from Mexico's border towns flooded into Texas by the thousands. The hope and pride the Mexican Revolution generated for Mexicans served as a catalyst for Mexican Americans in South Texas to assert themselves against the politically dominant Anglos; the forceful response left a bitter legacy.

Two days after he escaped from a Mexican prison in 1910, Francisco Madero crossed the Rio Grande at Laredo, Texas, headed for San Antonio. Mexicans along the border and in San Antonio received him enthusiastically. To avoid violating American neutrality laws and to protect supporters still in Mexico, Madero denied any intentions of using Texas as a base to organize a revolution, but he secretly began preparing the financial, military, and ideological foundation for a revolt against the dictatorship of Porfirio Díaz. In 1911 Madero launched his successful revolution against Díaz.

As rebel activity had intensified, American officials had begun to worry over violation of their neutrality laws. U.S. marshals, customs officers, and army troops were sent to patrol the border, but they found little evidence to support charges of flagrant rebel activity. On March 6, 1911, President William Howard Taft ordered twenty thousand troops to the U.S.–Mexico border, ostensibly for overdue military maneuvers

General Pancho Villa established headquarters in an El Paso office building during the Mexican Revolution. He directed a massive flow of supplies from the United States to Mexican troops via rail through the border city. He is shown seated on the left, with General Pascual Orozco at the same table, at the Elite Confectionery in El Paso in 1911. Courtesy of the Southwest Collection, El Paso Public Library.

to test the army's ability to respond to a crisis.

After General Victoriano Huerta overthrew Madero in 1913, Madero's followers, led by Venustiano Carranza, emptied shelves of every kind of ammunition in stores along the border from Brownsville to El Paso. They purchased rifles by the thousands and ammunition by the millions of rounds as they prepared to renew their revolution. By the spring of 1913, the fighting reached the Rio Grande, where opposing armies fought for control of the border towns.

Carranza overthrew Huerta in 1914, only to be challenged by Francisco (Pancho) Villa for the presidency of Mexico. From his headquarters in Ciudad Juárez and with supplies largely acquired from El Paso, Villa organized his revolution against the Carranza government. After failing to win American support for his revolutionary movement, in the spring of 1916 Villa turned on Americans along the border. He attacked Columbus, New Mexico, and American soldiers led by General John Pershing tracked him into northern Mexico but failed to engage him. Villa had hoped to lure the American army so deeply into Mexico that war with the Carranza regime would result. Probably only the American entrance into World War I in Europe prevented this from happening.

The series of revolutions brought a new ideological fervor to the Texas border towns. Many Mexican Americans in South Texas began to rebel against the dominant class, mostly Anglo-Americans, who had displaced Mexican Americans from their lands and who held the political and economic power to make that displacement permanent. Led by social revolutionists Aniceto Pizaña and Luis de la Rosa, they launched seventy-three raids against railroad lines, bridges, and irrigation pumping stations, all symbols of Anglo permanency. Rebel bands ranging in size from ten to one hundred men robbed stores and small farms, recruited men, wounded several Anglo-Americans, and killed twenty-five, all of whom were accused of having mistreated the local Mexican-American population. The raids proved less significant than they might have, and the raiders brought the economy of South Texas to a standstill for only one year. They disturbed, but did not destroy, Anglo-American ranches and infrastructure.

The Mexican-American population in South Texas paid for the forays with lives and property. Even those who had taken no part in the revolt lived in fear for their lives because every Mexican American became a suspected raider or sympathizer, and law officials offered little quarter to either. In 1915 the killing of Mexican Americans along the border became so common that many of the deaths were never even reported. Perhaps as many as three thousand to five thousand persons lost their lives in the turmoil.

☆ Material on the relations between Texas and the Mexican Revolution was supplied by Rodolfo Rocha, associate professor of history at Pan American University. You can learn more about this subject by reading *Blood on the Border: The United States Army and the Mexican Irregulars* by Clarence Clendenen (New York: Macmillan, 1969).

The Terrell Election Laws of 1903 and 1905 requiring Texas voters to pay a poll tax before they could register to vote each year effectively prevented many Texans from voting. The citizen who paid this 1934 poll tax of $1.75 was fortunate, given the financial strains of the Great Depression. Courtesy of the Austin–Travis County Collection, Austin History Center, Austin Public Library.

The Terrell Election Laws

As the twentieth century dawned, a new era opened for electoral politics in Texas. The "Solid South" was being born, and the Democratic party was ready to consolidate power in the state. Moreover, a move was afoot to effectively deprive blacks of the vote they had so recently gained.

The pattern of politics to that point had been somewhat different than elsewhere in the states of the former Confederacy. Partly because the proportion of the population that was black—just under a quarter in 1880, less than a fifth by 1910—was smaller than in other southern states, the Democratic party could tolerate opposition parties more easily. In the two decades after Reconstruction, Texas Democrats faced strong challenges from discontented farmers who joined the Greenback and Populist parties. Texas blacks, under the skillful leadership of Norris Wright Cuney of Galveston, regularly voted for the Republicans and for third parties.

After 1896 the Populists virtually disappeared from Texas, leaving the Democrats the undisputed moguls of Texas politics. In November, 1902, voters approved a poll-tax amendment to their constitution, which the Democrats presented as a white-supremacy measure. Democrats had made repeated efforts to enact laws restricting the suffrage, but since white Democrats from "black belt" counties (those with large numbers of blacks) had less power in Texas than elsewhere, the state did not enact the poll tax until twenty-seven years after it was first proposed. Proponents of the poll tax argued that the restriction would eliminate "irresponsible" voters. Voting was not a natural right, they contended, but a privilege the state should extend only to those willing to commit themselves by paying the tax.

Alexander Watkins Terrell, a lawyer, plantation operator, farmer, Confederate general, state legislator, and U.S. minister to Turkey (1893–97), was the most prominent and constant advocate of the poll tax in Texas. In 1903 Terrell returned to the legislature to author the first of what became known as the Terrell election laws. That law, together with a more comprehensive statute passed two years later and also written by Terrell, in accordance with the new constitutional amendment, provided for a noncumulative poll tax to be paid six months before each election. This stipulation effectively reduced the size of the electorate and removed many blacks, Mexican Americans, and poor whites from the political process.

The Terrell election laws also institutionalized the party primary system in Texas. They required a statewide nominating primary for all state, district, and county officials for any party polling more than 100,000 votes in the previous election. As the Democratic party grew in strength, its nomination became virtual assurance of election to office. But the party controlled "membership" and participation in the primaries, and eventually the Democrats denied membership and thus, for all intents, the vote to blacks. The white primary effectively, if only temporarily, disfranchised Texas blacks.

Terrell's laws—with adjustments such as the second, or runoff, primary instituted later—constitute the basic framework of the state's present election laws. The poll tax and the white primary, however, have been eliminated as a result of Federal court orders.

Taken together, the Terrell election laws also sealed the doom of opposition parties in Texas until the 1950s. The Democratic party became the only serious forum for the discussion and resolution of economic and social questions facing the state, and the institutionalizing of the one-party system after 1900 caused the Democrats to lapse into factionalism. In 1911 Governor Oscar B. Colquitt commented wryly, "We have only one political party in Texas but there are enough political fights in that one for half a dozen."

☆ This information on the Terrell election laws was provided by Norman D. Brown, professor of history at the University of Texas at Austin. You can learn more about this era by reading Alwyn Barr, *Reconstruction to Reform: Texas Politics, 1876–1906* (Austin: University of Texas Press, 1971).

United Mine Workers joined brickmakers, carpenters, clerks, meat cutters, bartenders, and even unskilled laborers to make the Palo Pinto County town of Thurber a "100 percent union town" in 1903. Courtesy of Special Collections, the University of Texas at Arlington Library.

Texas Labor

Individualism runs strong in the veins of Texas culture and has often been blamed for—or credited with—the relative lack of strength of labor unions in Texas. Ironically, though, one of the most fascinating strikes in the state's history was staged by the very symbol of rugged individualism, the cowboy. In the 1800s Texas cowboys in Panhandle region organized to protest their low wages of thirty dollars a month, poor working conditions, a work day of twelve to eighteen hours, and bad food, or "chuck" as they called it. More than three hundred cowboys stopped working in one of the few cowboy strikes in American history. However, the cowboys squandered much of their "strike fund" on drinking and gambling in Tascosa, and they refused to use force against other men entering the territory looking for work. The strike collapsed in a few weeks.

Organizations of laborers, mostly benevolent associations, had operated in Texas before the American Civil War, but true labor unions did not emerge until after the war, when they arose in response to expanding business, particularly in shipping, railroading, and manufacturing. In 1866 a group of stevedores, or longshoremen, in Galveston organized themselves into a benevolent association that was a true union, and in 1870 an association of black longshoremen formed there under the leadership of Norris Wright Cuney. Houston, Galveston, and Austin had locals of the International Typographical Union in the 1870s. The United Mine Workers operated in Texas in the coal mines in Erath and Palo Pinto counties after 1884. Some Texans joined the National Labor Union and the Knights of Labor, but because these organizations had individual membership rather than a pyramid structure of local, state, and international affiliations and because they preferred a legislative route rather than strikes to improve the workers' lot, they proved largely ineffective.

At about the time the Panhandle cowboys were organizing, railroad baron Jay Gould, who bragged that he could hire half the working class to kill the other half, controlled a third of the railroads in Texas and was the biggest employer in the Southwest. Railroad employees worked a seven-day week at an average wage of less than two dollars a day. In 1886 Gould cut wages and refused to recognize the workers' union. His actions led to the Great Southwest Strike, when nine thousand southwestern railroad hands, five thousand of them in Texas, walked out. The peaceful beginnings of the strike gave way to violence in the Battle of Buttermilk Switch in Fort Worth. Jim Courtright, who was not only acting city marshal but also a gunman for the Missouri Pacific Railroad, shot several picketers, and one of his deputies was killed. The strike was finally broken by state militia, federal deputies who were also in the pay of the companies, and the availability of cheap replacement laborers.

When the spirit of reform swept the state in the early twentieth century, Texas labor took up several progressive causes. Unions lobbied successfully for free textbooks for public school students, the abolition of the notorious convict lease system, and workers' safety laws. Hard times came again for labor, though, during the open-shop drives of the 1920s and the Depression of the 1930s. Ladies' garment workers were paid five to ten dollars a week for long hours in hot, dirty shops. In many shops they could not even use the bathroom except during their thirty-minute lunch breaks. In 1935 Dallas garment manufacturers' refusal to bargain with their union precipitated a strike in which non-union working women dumped hair-set lotion and trash on the picketers and the pickets stripped the clothes off several women workers who crossed their lines. The strikers were blacklisted and easily replaced.

In San Antonio Mexican-American pecan shellers made about two dollars for a fifty-hour work week in poorly ventilated, unsanitary factories. Faced with a sudden 15 percent wage cut in 1938, some twelve thousand of them walked out. Dozens were clubbed and beaten. The strike ended when the federal minimum-wage law made it more profitable for the pecan-shelling industry to automate than to pay their workers legal wages. Most workers lost their jobs, but the unionized shellers who remained enjoyed better wages, hours, and working conditions than the industry had ever known.

Of course, in all periods of history, even in the late nineteenth century and the Great Depression, a large majority of labor-management differences have been settled peacefully and without resorting to either strikes by labor or lockouts by management. Recently, new concerns such as the efforts by the Texas AFL-CIO to organize public employees and attempts to persuade the legislature to grant collective bargaining rights to the public sector have arisen. Organized labor also expresses worries about the hundreds of thousands of undocumented workers who have crossed the border since World War II. Usually these people take lower-paying jobs that are not coveted by native workers, but no doubt some have displaced Americans in higher-paying trades. While still concerned with wages, hours, and conditions, the modern labor movement is also active in civic endeavors and cooperative ventures with management.

☆ These facts on labor unions in Texas were provided by George N. Green, professor of history at the University of Texas at Arlington. The Texas AFL-CIO in 1982 published Professor Green's *The Heritage of Texas Labor,* which you might consult for more details.

Minnie Fisher Cunningham and Lone Star Suffrage

The women gathered in front of the town's most notorious brothel. Armed with cameras, they photographed both practitioners and patrons as they entered the establishment. If customers refused to leave they took photographs of their automobile license plates. Minnie Fisher Cunningham's "White Zone Campaigners" had struck again. Armed with their pictures, they marched to city hall to demand enforcement of ordinances against prostitution and other sins.

Like many others who worked to secure the vote for women, Cunningham developed her political activism from a range of civic and social concerns. Obtaining the vote was both a means to enacting a social reform agenda and a right whose intrinsic importance was particularly clear to those with heightened political awareness.

Minnie Fisher was born in New Waverly, Texas, on March 19, 1882. Her father, a plantation owner, former Confederate offi-

In March, 1918, Gov. William Hobby signed a bill granting most Texas women the right to vote in primary elections. Women in Austin (shown here) and across the state hurried to courthouses to register before the primary registration deadline. Suffragist Minnie Fisher Cunningham wrote to a friend, "I registered today. And honey, you'll never know how I felt when I walked out with that piece of paper. But I know how a mocking bird feels when he perches on the top most swaying bough. . . ." Courtesy of the Austin History Center, Austin Public Library (PICA 11669).

cer, and politician, insisted that she be educated and that she follow the teachings of Methodism. Observing her father's career, she also acquired a love for politics. She graduated from the pharmacy program at the University of Texas Medi-

cal Branch at Galveston in 1901 and practiced her profession for a year in Conroe before marrying Beverly Jean Cunningham, a lawyer and insurance executive. The marriage eventually failed.

After the hurricane of 1900, Cunningham joined Galveston's efforts to rebuild, especially to improve its health and sanitary facilities. Her civic involvement led her to join a group of women holding meetings about the rights of women. She grew increasingly active in the statewide suffrage campaign and in 1915 was elected president of the state suffrage association. Her tenacious debating abilities served the cause well and were used to help gain the impeachment of the state's leading foe of suffrage, Gov. James Ferguson. Her organizational skills and tireless stumping of the state bore fruit in 1918 when Governor William P. Hobby signed a constitutional amendment that allowed women to vote in primary elections, giving them an effective voice in party politics two years before the Nineteenth Amendment to the U.S. Constitution enfranchised the women of the nation. In a one-party state, where primaries almost always decided the real contest, this was more than a token victory.

Cunningham served as state chairman of the women's Liberty Loan Committee during World War I. Struggling to defend the purity of America's young men who trained in Texas, she organized the Texas Women's Anti-Vice Committee to demand an end to liquor traffic and prostitution near military training camps.

The success of the state primary suffrage movement brought Cunningham to the attention of Carrie Chapman Catt, president of the National American Woman Suffrage Association. Catt invited Cunningham to serve as the secretary of the association's congressional committee in Washington. Cunningham focused the lobbying techniques she had used so effectively in Texas

on the members of Congress. After the passage of the Nineteenth Amendment, Cunningham became the executive secretary of the National League of Women Voters.

Cunningham entered party politics in 1923, becoming executive secretary of the Women's National Democratic Club and editor of the *Democratic Bulletin*. She conducted training schools for newly enfranchised women voters, and Eleanor Roosevelt was one of the young voters enrolled in Cunningham's classes.

In 1927 Cunningham announced her candidacy for the U.S. Senate against the Texas incumbent, Earle B. Mayfield. The first woman in Texas to run for the office, Cunningham focused the attention of the voters on farm relief, prohibition, and an adequate flood-control program. She openly opposed the Ku Klux Klan at a time when the state generally favored the secret organization. Cunningham placed fifth in a field of six candidates in the Democratic primary.

She joined the Texas Agricultural Extension Service at Texas A. & M. College in 1930 as associate editor and later as editor. In 1939 she returned to Washington as an information specialist in the Women's Division of the Agricultural Adjustment Administration. She served until 1943, when she resigned in protest of a gag rule imposed on all departmental employees.

Returning to Texas once more, Cunningham announced her candidacy for the office of governor. Her campaign was based upon her promise to give full support to the war effort. She attacked Governor Coke Stevenson's obstruction of the federal gasoline rationing program and his cuts in old age pensions to decrease the state deficit. A maverick politician, Cunningham ran the first independent gubernatorial campaign by a woman in the state's history. Despite a vigorous campaign, she lost in the primary by a large margin.

Even though Cunningham gave up the quest for public office, she continued to fight for reforms in the governmental system. In 1944, Cunningham and Jane Y. McCallum, former secretary of state of Texas, formed the Women's Committee for Educational Freedom, which publicly opposed the conservative policies of Gov. Coke R. Stevenson. The committee came to the defense of Homer P. Rainey, former president of the University of Texas, who had been fired in 1944 for defending academic freedom. In 1946, the organization supported Rainey's bid for the governorship. In 1944 Cunningham helped found the Democrats of Texas, a liberal state Democratic organization. In the 1950s, she organized the Texas Democratic Women's State Committee.

Seeking a wider platform for her ideas, Cunningham began to write a column for the liberal *State Observer*. In 1954 she brought together liberal friends from across the state to save the newspaper from a conservative buyer. She offered to mortgage part of her 1,200-acre Fisher Farms to complete the purchase of the paper. The *Texas Observer* emerged out of her efforts and those of her friends. She became a heroine for embattled Texas liberals throughout the 1950s. Until her death in 1964 she remained capable of peppering opponents in debate. Her life dramatized the opening of political opportunity to women brought by the vote.

☆ Details concerning Minnie Fisher Cunningham's contributions were provided by John Carroll Eudy, instructor in history at North Harris County Community College. You can read about women's suffrage in Eleanor Flexner's *Century of Struggle: The Women's Rights Movement in the United States* (Cambridge: Harvard University Press, 1975).

Ma Ferguson Takes on the Klan

"I don't know much about politics, but I do know that my Redeemer liveth!" Thus began the colorful political career of Mrs. Miriam A. ("Ma") Ferguson in 1924. Her husband, James A. Ferguson (called "Farmer Jim" and later "Pa"), had won the governorship in 1914, running as a neo-populist.

His administration had featured the passage of a farm-tenant rent law, later declared unconstitutional, which fixed share rates, a law providing for consolidation of rural high schools, compulsory school attendance, and free text books, and the creation of the Texas Highway Department.

Ferguson's administration ended in 1917 amid charges of misuse of state funds and other transgressions. Lieutenant Governor William P. Hobby succeeded Ferguson and won reelection in 1918. In 1920 Pat Neff gained election to the first of two terms.

As a post–World War I crime wave hit Texas, the revived Ku Klux Klan, which appeared in the state late in 1920, stood for "law and order" (as it understood the term), for the enforcement of Prohibition, and against corrupt officialdom. The hooded order undertook a campaign of intimidation and violence—whipping, tar-and-feathering, and sometimes branding—aimed primarily at bootleggers, gamblers, adulterers, wife beaters, and other moral offenders. From 1922 to 1924 the Klan became the paramount issue in Texas politics as the organization elected city and county officeholders, legislators, and, in 1922, U.S. Senator Earle B. Mayfield. Klansmen boasted that Texas was, politically speaking, the banner Klan state in the nation.

Mrs. Miriam A. Ferguson, a housewife and mother, made a race for governor of Texas in 1924 as a proxy for her husband because he had been barred from holding state office by his impeachment conviction. Despite his fall from political grace, the charismatic Jim Ferguson retained the vest-pocket vote of thousands of tenant farmers, owners of small farms, and day laborers—the "boys at the forks of the creek."

Mrs. Ferguson faced a Klan-backed candidate, Judge Felix Robertson of Dallas, in the Democratic runoff primary. After she

"Vote for Ma and you get two governors for the price of one!" supporters of Miriam "Ma" Ferguson and her husband, Jim, told voters. Each Ferguson served two terms as governor. Jim Ferguson (to the right of Gov. Miriam Ferguson) also directed state affairs during his wife's term of office. Courtesy of the Austin History Center, Austin Public Library (CO 2896).

agreed to pose for campaign photographs wearing a sunbonnet, Texas voters were offered the choice of "a bonnet or a hood." New lyrics were composed to fit "Ma's" campaign song, "Put on Your Old Gray Bonnet":

> Get out your old time bonnet
> And put Miriam Ferguson on it.
>   And hitch your wagon to a star.

So on election day
We each of us can say
   Hurrah! Governor Miriam, Hurrah!

Mrs. Ferguson's runoff victory by a margin of nearly a hundred thousand votes signaled the demise of the Klan as a force in Texas politics. "It was all over," recalled a former Klansman. "After Robertson was beaten the prominent men left the Klan. The Klan's standing went with them."

The Fergusons' career continued long after the Klan disappeared as an important political force in the state, but it was a checkered career. Mrs. Ferguson, though one of the first two women governors in the nation, was governor in name only. Her husband's office was next to hers, and his presence—real or felt—dominated her meetings and decisions. She was defeated for reelection in 1926 by Attorney General Dan Moody, after an administration marred by scandal in the granting of highway contracts and widespread criticism of her liberal pardoning policy. Nonetheless, she won a second term as governor in 1932 during the depths of the Great Depression, narrowly defeating incumbent Ross S. Sterling. The Fergusons ran—and lost—their last race in 1940, when Mrs. Ferguson challenged anti–New Deal Governor W. Lee ("Pappy") O'Daniel and finished fourth in the first primary. The bonnet then followed the hood into the realm of things past.

☆ These facts about the Fergusons and the Klan come from Norman D. Brown, professor of history at the University of Texas at Austin. Professor Brown's fascinating book *Hood, Bonnet, and Little Brown Jug: Texas Politics, 1921–1928* (College Station: Texas A&M University Press, 1984) will tell you more about these colorful figures in the state's history.

Hispanic Theater

European drama was first performed in Texas by the soldiers and settlers of Juan de Oñate's colonizing expedition from Mexico in 1598, at a site not far from today's city of El Paso. Spanish-language theater has graced Texas and the Southwest since that time. In the early twentieth century it reached its pinnacle, as Texas became a home for thousands of immigrants seeking refuge from the upheavals of the Mexican Revolution.

Mexican theater in Texas in the 1920s ranged from opera and serious drama in magnificent theater houses to slapstick under a canvas tent. But vaudeville was king: a popular potpourri of circus and musical-comedy acts and social satire. Staged in the finest theaters, as well as in the shabbiest of circus tents, it starred glamorous, bejeweled divas alongside the most raggedy, comic hoboes imaginable.

On the vaudeville stage, the *revista*, a loose satirical one-act skit that involved song, dance, and comedy, provided a lively form of social commentary. *Revistas* blended the divergent styles of operetta with tent-theater clowning; many featured librettos written by the most talented Mexican playwrights. The *revista* had developed in Mexico as a format for piquant political commentary and the airing of grievances. In Texas, the *revista* and other comedy sketches highlighted the language, customs, humor, and preoccupations of Mexicans within a new culture and environment. In the hands of such accomplished comics as La Chata Noloesca or Leonardo García Astol, it became the popular medium in which a new Mexican-American identity first appeared.

No performer knew the community better or was better able to create joy out of adversity, especially during the Depression, than Beatriz La Chata Noloesca. At San Antonio's famed Teatro Nacional, Beatriz Noloesca worked her way up from ticket girl in the box office to chorus girl and ultimately became the most beloved comedienne of the Hispanic stage in the United States. Her career took her and her family from the Alamo City to New York City, to the Caribbean, and to Latin America. Years later she retired in San Antonio and took her final bow in 1979. Her daughter, Belia Areu, who had followed in her footsteps, remains an active performer in Texas.

The Mexican-American stage has helped to solidify the sense of Hispanic community by bringing its divergent segments together in a cultural act, the preservation and support of the language and the art of Mexicans and other *hispanos* in the face of domination by a foreign culture.

San Antonio's Beatriz "La Chata" Noloesca (center) left the chorus line and worked her way to the top in Hispanic comedy in the United States. Here she is shown in a skit at New York's Teatro Hispano. Courtesy of Arte Publico Press and the San Antonio Conservation Society.

☆ Nicolás Kanellos, professor of Hispanic and classical languages at the University of Houston, gave this information on the Mexican theater in Texas. He has written a book, *Mexican American Theatre: Then and Now* (Houston: Arte Publico Press, 1983), from which you can learn much more on the subject.

Texas Rangers versus Bonnie and Clyde

The job of a Texas Ranger in the 1930s was awesome. Armed with "one improved carbine" he had bought "at cost" from the state, the Ranger faced a plethora of gangsters who procured at no cost—and seldom hesitated to use—Thompson submachine guns and Browning automatic rifles. While criminals in high-powered automobiles "shuttled between distant cities like commuters," the Rangers had to rely on free railroad passes or provide their own automobiles on a monthly allotment of fifty dollars per company for "repairs and upkeep."

Clearly, the Texas Rangers, although benefiting from the excellent leadership of Adjutant General William W. "Bill" Sterling, were seriously handicapped in 1931. The Great Depression had caused the state legislature to slash their budget, and the Rangers, who at full complement had numbered seventy-five men, counted only thirty-five to forty-five officers. Besides being understaffed, they also followed antiquated procedures, which had not kept pace with modern science and urbanization.

Then, to make matters worse, in July, 1932, the Rangers made a grave error in judgment, openly supporting Governor Ross Sterling against Miriam A. "Ma" Ferguson in the Democratic primary. After assuming office in January, 1933, Governor Ferguson charged all forty-four Rangers on active duty with partisanship and fired them, despite their commendable record of law enforcement. The state legislature also reduced Ranger salaries, eliminated longevity pay, slashed budgets, and limited the force to thirty-two men. Mrs. Ferguson appointed new officers, many of whom were a "contemptible lot" by any standard. Even worse, she began granting Special Ranger commissions as a source of political patronage. Within two years she had swelled the number of Rangers to 2,344 men. The *Austin American* was prompted to comment that "about all the requirements a person needed . . . to be a Special Ranger was to be a human Being."

These changes had catastrophic consequences for state law enforcement. And who besides "Ma" Ferguson was responsible for the breakdown in public defense? To most Texans the answer was obvious. As one newspaper editor sarcastically remarked, "A Ranger commission and a nickel can get . . . a cup of coffee anywhere in Texas." During the Ferguson years crime and violence in Texas were widespread, and bank holdups and murder dramatically increased. Soon few states hosted a more vicious assortment of gangsters or provide a safer sanctuary for the criminal element. Residents in the Dallas–Fort Worth area alone included George "Machine Gun" Kelly, Raymond Hamilton, and "mad-dog killers" Clyde Barrow and Bonnie Parker.

Clyde Barrow and Bonnie Parker were the most wanted outlaws in Texas in the 1930s. In January, 1934, near Huntsville, they killed a prison guard while helping four convicts to escape. Near Grapevine in April they brutally murdered two

CLYDE CHAMPION BARROW, age 24, 5'7",130#,hair dark brown and
wavy,eyes hazel,light complexion,home West Dallas,Texas.
This man killed Detective Harry McGinnis and Constable
J.W. Harryman in this city,April 13, 1933.

BONNIE PARKER CLYDE BARROW   CLYDE BARROW

This man is dangerous and is known to have committed the following
murders: Howard Hall, Sherman, Texas; J.N.Bucher,Hillsboro, Texas;
a deputy sheriff at Atoka, Okla; deputy sheriff at West Dallas,
Texas; also a man at Belden, Texas.
    The above photos are kodaks taken by Barrow and his com-
panions in various poses,and we believe they are better for
identification than regular police pictures.
    Wire or write any information to the

                Police Department.

Because he had murdered several law officers, bank robber Clyde Barrow was the object of a massive interstate manhunt. Former Texas Ranger Frank Hamer led the team that intercepted Barrow in May, 1934, on a Louisiana side road, killing him and his companion, Bonnie Parker. Courtesy of the Moody Texas Ranger Library, Waco, Texas.

highway patrolmen who had approached their parked car on the highway to offer assistance. Their ruthless murders continued until the death toll rose to fifteen.

Because the best law enforcement officers in Texas were no longer Rangers, Lee Simmons, superintendent of the Texas prison system, persuaded former Ranger Captain Frank Hamer to accept a commission as a highway patrolman with the assignment of tracking down Barrow and Parker. Hamer took up the trail on February 10, 1934. He learned everything he could about the outlaws, including their habits, their routine, and their physical and mental makeup. He soon observed that they "played a circle from Dallas to Joplin, Missouri, to Louisiana, and back to Dallas." So after recruiting former Ranger B. M. "Manny" Gault and Dallas sheriff's department deputies Bob Alcorn and Ted Hinton to help him, Hamer contacted Sheriff Henderson Jordan of Bienville Parish, Louisiana, and one of his deputies. Together the six men set an ambush at the gangsters' "post office," a designated place where their mail was dropped on a lonely side road some eight miles from Plain Dealing, Louisiana. At 9:20 A.M. on May 23, 1934, Clyde Barrow and Bonnie Parker stopped at their pick-up spot. Their car was idling at a complete stop. When commanded to "stick 'em up," they reached for their weapons. A deadly barrage riddled the car, instantly killing Parker and Barrow.

Although not then in the Ranger service, Captain Hamer enhanced the Ranger tradition. He had bravely, even doggedly, tracked the two most feared desperados in the state. And in the Ranger tradition of brief reports to superiors, he sent the following account of his 102-day mission to Superintendent Simmons: "I done the job."

☆ Ben Procter, professor of history at Texas Christian University, provided this information. If you want to know more about this era in Ranger history, you can go to *I'm Frank Hamer: The Life of a Texas Peace Officer* by H. Gordon Frost and John H. Jenkins (Austin: Pemberton Press, 1968).

Texas' Grapes of Wrath

"Farms ain't farms no more; not no real business," complained Sam Tucker, the tenant farmer—hero of George Sessions Perry's novel *Hold Autumn in Your Hand* (1941). The Dust Bowl and the New Deal's agricultural policies had touched a way of life that went way back in Texas history. Until then, backbreaking labor, long hours in the hot sun, and fervent prayers for seasonable weather had gone into trying to keep up with the nation's fast-growing demand for food and cotton. All at once, the boom went bust, and farmers were the first to feel the new squeeze.

Even by the end of World War I, Texas farming was no longer frontier agriculture.

When Depression-era cotton prices plunged to a new low, some tenant farmers had to leave their home fields and take day-labor jobs on larger mechanized cotton farms. Farm Security Administration photographer Arthur Rothstein spoke with these Kaufman County workers in 1936 as their pickings were weighed and found that they received fifty cents per hundred pounds. Courtesy of the Library of Congress.

The land was fenced and plowed; rural communities lent conveniences and stability to farm life; and the wartime demand for agricultural products had created unprecedented prosperity.

Prices had increased dramatically, and farm jobs were plentiful. However, overproduction caused a sharp price break in 1920–21, and although a rise in cotton prices from 1922 to 1925 muted agrarian discontent, it did not solve the farmers' basic problems. These stemmed from unscientific agriculture, the crop-lien system, tenancy, a less than satisfactory marketing system, and overproduction.

From 1919 to 1926 Texas increased its

cotton acreage from something over 10 million acres to over 18 million acres, and its production rose from 3 million bales to almost 6 million bales. Prices dropped again in 1926, and after the Great Depression descended, Texas farmers' cotton sold for five cents per pound or less. Farmers hauled cotton to the gin only to discover that they could not even pay the ginning costs with what they got for their crops. Rather than take it home again, many farmers dumped the cotton along the roads to rot. In some areas it was more economical to burn corn for fuel than to buy firewood.

The tenant farmer working on shares stood near the bottom of the Texas agricultural pyramid. By 1920 just over half of all Texas farmers were tenants, and nearly two out of three farmers in the nineteen "blackland" counties worked other people's land. "My father's father was a sharecropper," novelist William Humphrey wrote in his memoir, *Farther Off from Heaven*, published in 1977. "To the end, going blind with cataracts and feeling his way with his feet in the furrows, my grandfather clung to his dream of gathering a good enough crop for a couple of years in succession to make a down payment on a place of his own and 'work for himself.' Instead, the gathering of his crop and its sale, the one time of the year when he held cash money in his hand, often left him in debt to the owner of the crossroads store for what he had advanced them to keep alive on." Tenant farming posed a social problem that only the restructuring of the agricultural economy finally "solved."

The New Deal's agricultural program sought to address the problem of overproduction of staple crops such as cotton by signing contracts with farmers to limit their acreage in exchange for government payments. In the first year, farmers who signed these contracts were required to plow under from one-fourth to one-half of their growing crops. This plan for attaining prosperity through destruction puzzled many people. Perry's fictional character Sam Tucker expressed this bewilderment, saying that farms had become "just reservations where the government gives men money to stay there and keep off relief. Reservations to stay on and raise somethin' that you and the government plays like there's some use for. An it seems strange when you know this year's cotton'll be just as good, just as white, an better staple than it ever was; just as much work to raise. Except there ain't no use for but about half of it."

The Dust Bowl developed in northwest Texas, western Oklahoma, Kansas, and Nebraska, in the 1930s, where the grassy covering of the prairies had been destroyed. Then, exceptional drought killed off much of the remaining groundcover, and winds swept the soil away. The worst soil-blowing storms occurred from 1933 to 1936. During this period, Texas contributed significantly to the so-called Okie migration of homeless people to California, portrayed with compassion and understanding in John Steinbeck's famous novel *The Grapes of Wrath*. Prosperity did not return to Texas farmers until the demands of World War II once again made agricultural work profitable.

 This information on the plight of Depression-era farmers in Texas was provided by Norman D. Brown, professor of history at the University of Texas at Austin. If you want to learn more about the beginnings of this difficult period, you could read *The Depression in Texas: The Hoover Years* (New York: Garland, 1983).

Singer of the Poor

The Depression of the 1930s affected everyone in Texas, but it was an especially difficult time for Mexican Americans. Most of them worked in low-paying jobs in agriculture and industry, and when layoffs became necessary, they usually were the first to go. Since many were recent immigrants from Mexico and thus were considered foreign labor, their presence was resented by Anglo and black Texans, who saw Mexican Americans working in jobs that they wanted for themselves. So Mexican Americans often became scapegoats for the economic problems that affected everyone. Many were forcibly "repatriated"; even some who were born in the United States were illegally deported to Mexico. Families were disrupted, and many workers who escaped deportation were unemployed. As a result, poverty, hunger, and unhappiness dominated the "barrios," or Mexican neighborhoods. With prejudice against Mexican Americans at an all-time high, they were listed as "colored" on the census forms in 1930.

One family well illustrates the burdens borne by Mexican Americans in Texas during the Depression, although their rise from poverty makes them somewhat exceptional. The Mendoza family—including Francisco Mendoza, his wife Leonora,

their daughters Lydia and Panchita, and several other children—turned to music as a solace for their troubles. They began to perform for other Mexican Americans—for pay—and eventually Lydia achieved widespread popularity and good compensation. Francisco played the tambourine, his wife the guitar, Lydia the mandolin, and Panchita the triangle; and the entire family sang to the accompaniment of their instruments. As the younger children grew old enough to sing or play an instrument, they were added to the group.

The Mendoza family began their musical career in 1927 by giving performances on Saturdays in barbershops and restaurants in the Rio Grande Valley to earn money to supplement their wages in order to survive. Mostly they performed for other Mexican Americans. Then they decided to join a migrant-worker crew bound for Michigan to harvest beets. After arriving in Michigan, they found that they could make more money playing music for their friends than they could working in the fields. They played in restaurants in Detroit and Pontiac, Michigan. Francisco Mendoza even found a job in an automobile assembly plant, and for a time the family finances showed a surplus.

When the market crash of 1929 made

Young Lydia Mendoza and her family gained a wide audience during radio broadcasts of their musical performances in San Antonio during the 1930s. She remains a popular entertainer on the folk music circuit in the 1980s. Courtesy of the *San Antonio Light* Collection, the University of Texas Institute of Texan Cultures, San Antonio.

the automobile industry uncertain, and especially as the Depression intensified, the Mendoza family suffered. Few Mexican Americans had the funds to pay them for playing their music, and the father lost his job. The family had to sell their possessions in 1931, and they moved to San Antonio. Unable to find work, Mendoza every evening took his family to the Plaza del Zacate, or Haymarket Square, where they would play for pennies. At the low point of their circumstances, Leonora collected dead pigeons off the street to cook for their meals.

Then good fortune rescued the Mendozas from their poverty. Lydia Mendoza's singing in the plaza pleased a local radio announcer, who invited her to perform on his program. Soon she was singing and playing nightly on the Spanish-language radio show. She won a radio singing competition sponsored by the Pearl Beer Company, and she and her family were contracted to make recordings for Bluebird Records. In 1934 Lydia Mendoza's recording of "Mal Hombre" (No-good Man) became a hit. Soon her voice was recognized by Mexican Americans across the Southwest. The family was able to stop giving concerts in the plaza for pennies. They performed in clubs, theaters, and church halls in the barrios of Texas towns. By 1940 Lydia Mendoza and her family had recorded more than two hundred songs and frequently toured the Southwest to perform.

Lydia became known as "la cancionera de los pobres" (the singer of the poor), but not because she sang about poverty. Rather, her music, coming out of the Hispanic soul and expressing a shared cultural vision, offered those who were poor the solace that comes from being together and being one. She sang about her love for her mother, about dancing and having fun, about being betrayed by the "bad man" she loved, about children singing about death. Hearing these songs, people wept—for she expressed their life together where they were outsiders and forgotten. Struggling men and women spent precious money to buy Lydia's records so that they could have this experience again and again.

The Depression ended; prejudice eased. But Lydia Mendoza and her family had created music that lived within a culture and helped make that culture conscious; it would not grow old. Lydia Mendoza's music has lasted through generations and is still popular today; the soul of a people abides.

☆ Information on the Mendoza family was furnished by Dan W. Dickey, Latin American music specialist at the University of Texas at Austin. The description and assessment of Lydia Mendoza's music were provided by Frederick P. Close, director of the Southwest Center for Educational Television. You can still enjoy recordings of her songs made during the 1920s and 1930s: Folklyric Records #9023 and #9024, in the series "Texas-Mexican Border Music," volumes 15 and 16.

Governor Ross Sterling's proposal for daily allowable oil production limits met with bitterness among wildcatters in the Texas oilfields. Sterling called out the National Guard to restore order during the 1931 "Oil War" in East Texas. Courtesy of the East Texas Oil Museum, Kilgore, Texas.

The Hot Oil War

When the Daisy Bradford No. 3 came in, on October 5, 1930, many in the oil industry started looking for hats to eat. A "poor-boy" oil promoter, Columbus Marion ("Dad") Joiner, successfully completed this discovery well of the great East Texas oil field, to the shock and consternation of the oil industry. The giant companies, especially Humble Oil and Refining, the Shell Oil Company, and the Atlantic Oil Company, had assumed long before that the East Texas area lacked sufficient oil reserves to

131

justify commercial production, despite the fact that oil had been discovered in the region as early as 1866. Joiner's unsuccessful attempts to find oil in the Daisy Bradford No. 1 and No. 2 wells had seemed to confirm what the geologists employed by the large companies believed.

When the well came in, thousands of people rushed to Kilgore and other towns near the discovery well to find work, but the major oil companies did not invest there because they still believed that Joiner had found only an isolated pool. By the end of 1930, though, it was clear that what Joiner had hit was a large and prolific field. The Deep Rock Oil Company and the Bateman Oil Company, a Fort Worth independent, drilled successfully at considerable distances from Joiner's initial strike and found equally large quantities of high-grade oil that was easy and profitable to refine. In fact, Joiner had discovered the largest field in history.

By June, 1931, over 350,000 barrels of oil flowed daily from wells in the East Texas field, and that much oil glutted the already over-supplied market. Oil prices dropped to ten cents a barrel. Still, the independent oil producers who controlled the field continued to market their product.

The failure of the major oil companies to enter the competition for domination of the field had allowed hundreds of independent producers from Dallas, Fort Worth, and Houston to control it. Their dominance was made easier by the presence of a large number of small tracts of land owned by separate individuals. The independents would have had lots of opportunities to snatch leases out from under the

noses of the "big guys" even if the big companies had showed up to bid. As it was, the major companies did not enter the competition early, and they could never afterward secure enough leases to crowd out independents who were unwilling to sell.

Most independents, such as Joiner, were "poor-boy" operators who had to borrow money to drill their wells. With the discovery of such vast quantities, they could quickly repay their debts, even if their oil sold at ten cents per barrel. They could not afford to curtail their production no matter how it might have aided the economy.

By January, 1931, it became obvious that neither the oil producers nor the Texas Railroad Commission, the agency that had been given the responsibility of regulating the state's oil fields, could control excess production. The commission's orders were ignored by the independents, who continued to produce oil in excess of their daily allotment, or "daily allowable." Such oil was called "hot" because it was produced in violation of state regulations. The commission reasoned, pleaded, and threatened, but the oilmen continued to pump their oil.

A crisis was reached on August 16, 1931, following the commission's order that the field be partially shut down. Instead, production on that day reached one million barrels, a new record high. Governor Ross Sterling then ordered the Texas militia to close down the field and enforce the Railroad Commission's regulations.

The producers went to court, and a legal tangle resulted. The Federal courts prohibited the use of martial law in East Texas, but the Texas Court of Civil Appeals upheld the Railroad Commission's regulations. The "hot" oil continued to flow, and prices remained depressed.

The Federal government determined to settle the matter after the large oil companies and state governments had requested assistance in stopping the "hot" oil so that prices could rise. A provision of the National Industrial Recovery Act barred the sale of such oil in interstate commerce. When the NIRA was struck down by the U.S. Supreme Court, congressmen from Texas and Oklahoma supported legislation introduced by Senator Tom Connally of Texas to provide federal regulation of oil transactions in interstate commerce.

By the time the legislative solution to the problem of "hot" oil was achieved, the East Texas field had become more or less self-regulated. Wide-open production had led to the decline of production from wells on the edges of the field, and by 1935 the major oil companies had finally begun to buy out many of the independent producers. Oil is still pumped in the East Texas field, but since the 1930s, most of it has been produced within the boundaries of state and federal regulation.

☆ Roger M. Olien, professor of history at the University of Texas, Permian Basin, provided this information. You can learn more about the role of independent oilmen in a book he wrote with Diana Davids Olien, *Wildcatters: Texas Independent Oilmen* (Austin: Texas Monthly Press, 1984).

Texas Folk Music

Song may be to the soul of a people what breath is to the body. Perhaps the folk songs that have belonged most distinctively to the American people are black spirituals and cowboy ballads, and long nights on the Texas range have seen the birth of many a cowboy song.

John Avery Lomax is the best-known collector of Texas folk music, and the songs he is best known for are those he collected and published in 1910 in *Cowboy Songs and Other Frontier Ballads*. Lomax grew up in Bosque County along the Old Chisholm Trail, where he heard and learned cowboy songs. In 1906, his studies at Harvard made him aware of the importance of native Texas music, and he returned to Texas to collect the songs and to help establish in 1909 the Texas Folklore Society. The society later published his studies in folklore and folk music.

The songs John Lomax collected and preserved have become the cowboy classics:

I woke one morning on the Old Chisholm Trail
With a rope in my hand and a cow by the tail,
Come a ti yi yippe yippe yea, yippe yea
Come a ti yi yippe yippe yea.

Cowboys said that there were as many

133

verses to that song as there were miles on the trail.

The song that was reported to be President Franklin Roosevelt's favorite and which Admiral Richard Byrd carried with him to the South Pole was a song Lomax collected titled "Home on the Range."

> Oh give me a home where the buffalo roam,
> Where the deer and the antelope play,
> Where seldom is heard a discouraging word
> And the skies are not cloudy all day.
>
> CHORUS
> Home home on the range,
> Where the deer and the antelope play,
> Where seldom is heard a discouraging word,
> And the skies are not cloudy all day.

John Lomax's music crossed the color lines; he began collecting among penitentiary blacks in the 1930s, reasoning that individuals long isolated from ongoing cultural change would report songs in the least adulterated form. He visited The Walls, in Huntsville, and prison farms in Texas and Louisiana. His most notable discovery was a Texas-Louisiana black man named Huddie Ledbetter, usually called Leadbelly. After Lomax secured a parole for Leadbelly, the twelve-string guitar player worked as his chauffeur, helped him interview other black singers, and taught Lomax songs such as "The Midnight Special" that are still—thanks to Lomax's collecting—vital parts of Texas culture.

> If you ever go to Houston
> Boy, you better walk right;
> You better not gamble
> And you better not fight,

Folksong collector John Lomax might have been pausing in the middle of storytelling to light a cigar in this portrait. In the 1920s and 1930s he and his son drove to isolated towns and prisons in the South to record folksongs relatively uninfluenced by radio and phonograph records. Courtesy of the Barker Texas History Center, the University of Texas at Austin.

> Cause the sheriff will arrest you
> And throw you in jail.
> You can bet your bottom dollar,
> Ain't gonna be no bail.
>
> CHORUS
> Let the Midnight Special shine its light on me.
> Let the Midnight Special shine its ever lovin' light on me.

⭐ These facts about John Lomax and the music he collected come from Francis E. Abernethy, professor of English at Stephen F. Austin State University and secretary-editor of the Texas Folklore Society. Lomax revised and expanded his book, with Alan Lomax, in 1938; you can get it in any of several reprint editions from your library or local bookstore.

Texas as a Southern State

"Away here in Texas, the bright Sunny South," goes a line folklorist William Owens found in an 1844 edition of the Sacred Harp songbook. From the Old South, the music that accompanied these words had made its way to East Texas, where Owens was documenting traditional religious singing in the 1940s. It is one of many clues that Texan culture—lifestyle and literature alike—owes a big debt to the American South.

Even before statehood, most of the Anglo immigrants to Texas hailed from Kentucky, Tennessee, Missouri, and the mountain regions of Virginia and North Carolina. Later migrations flowed from Georgia, Alabama, Mississippi, Louisiana, and the Carolinas. For the most part, the newcomers continued to live and work as they had in the South. They farmed, plowing with mules; they grew cotton or sugar cane or corn; and, if they could afford it, they used slave labor—unless they came from an Upper South state and had learned that other labor sources were less expensive or less offensive.

Southerners came with a sense of history, of place and family, and with strong Protestant values, all of which strongly influenced Texas life. In the Old South—and in East Texas—the past lives, as it always has, in the oral records that families and communities pass down to younger members. The legends, tales, proverbs, and social laws continue to provide what writer William Humphrey calls "that feeling of identity with the dead which characterizes and explains the Southerner."

When the American Civil War began in 1861, there was little doubt about the sympathies of most Texans. A few, especially among German immigrants, opposed secession and affiliation with the Confederacy; most, however, welcomed separation from the Union and embraced the Southern Confederacy, which already included so many of their fellow Southerners. More than 60,000 Texas men served in the Confederate Army, including 135 who rose to the rank of general.

Following the war, still more Southerners poured into Texas looking for new starts, further binding the state to the Southern region for nearly a century. In politics the state was considered a part of the "Solid South" and strongly supported the Democratic party until recent years.

Although some Southerners who immigrated to Texas were Catholic, most were Protestant. The literary rhythms of the King James Bible and the pulpit rhetoric of old-style preachers can still be heard in white and black churches in East and Central Texas. These cadences and the evangelical theology of fundamentalist churches figure prominently in Texas folklore and fiction.

Books written in Texas, somewhat naturally, have reflected consciousness of the state's southernness. In his memoirs, *Farther Off from Heaven*, Humphrey described his departure from and eventual return to

Clarksville, Texas. "Just as the salmon must leave home when the time comes, so he must return to round out his life," Humphrey concluded. The significance of one's home place seems most acute in East Texas, where Southern influences remain strongest. Reflecting on his home town in northeast Texas, William Owens wrote, "Pin Hook is a part of me. All of my life has been a flight from it, but now, after many returnings, I see that it has overtaken me at last." With family ties so strong, community allegiances often prevail over loyalties to state and nation. Humphrey's and Owens's writings stand beside the fiction of Katherine Anne Porter, George Sessions Perry, and William Goyen, all natives of a Texas emerging from Southern influences earlier in the twentieth century.

Most of the folksongs collected in Owens's significant book *Texas Folksongs,* as well as the black blues of Leadbelly, Lightnin' Hopkins, and Manse Lipscomb, demonstrate the Southern roots of Texas folk music. Black folktales collected by J. Mason Brewer and the white legends and tales retold by J. Frank Dobie also show the influence of the Deep South on Texas folklore. And the careers of such Texas-born or Texas-based singers as Ernest Tubb, Bob Wills, and Willie Nelson attest to the southern "hillbilly" tradition in the state.

Place names in Texas also reflect its Southern heritage. Hundreds of towns, counties, streets, and schools are named for Robert E. Lee, Jefferson Davis, Stonewall Jackson, Jeb Stuart, Albert Sidney Johnston, and John Bell Hood. Monuments to Confederate soldiers dot scores

Texan William Goyen stands in front of the New Mexico home where he wrote the novel House of Breath *after World War II. Like many of his writings, it vividly portrayed southern culture and language and attracted European readers as well as Americans.* ©Doris Roberts and Charles William Goyen Trust. Used by permission. Courtesy of the Harry Ransom Humanities Research Center, the University of Texas at Austin.

of town squares and courthouse lawns. There is still, as in the Willie Nelson song, a window "that faces the South" in Texas.

☆ These insights into the southernness of Texas come from James W. Lee, professor of English at North Texas State University. You can learn more about the effects on Texas of immigration from the South, as well as ethnic immigration, in D. W. Meinig's outstanding interpretation of Texas culture, *Imperial Texas* (Austin: University of Texas Press, 1969).

Mr. Sam

"I am an old man of considerable power and I will not stay in this dump!" Reporters at the 1960 Democratic National Convention, the first convention that House Speaker Sam Rayburn had not chaired in nearly two decades, chuckled when "Mr. Sam" refused to stay in a second-class hotel near convention headquarters where the party hierarchy dominated by Senator John F. Kennedy had assigned him rooms. Rayburn had relinquished the gavel to lead the floor fight to gain the party's nomination for fellow Texan Lyndon Baines Johnson. He let it be known that he was still a man to be reckoned with, and Kennedy's supporters quickly found him rooms in the headquarters hotel.

Samuel Taliaferro Rayburn served in the U.S. House of Representatives for forty-eight years. At his death on November 16, 1961, he was perhaps the most revered man in Congress, the unquestioned leader of the House, the "teacher, tyrant, referee, and father to his changing brood of 434 congressmen." How did he earn such enormous respect? Rayburn's character, experience, and sound judgment all entered in. Through his knowledge and imaginative use of the House's rules, he was able to pass legislation and do other things that even some political experts considered impossible to accomplish. Regardless of political affiliation, he helped the president when he perceived national need to be involved and fiercely maintained that "I didn't serve under eight presidents. I served with eight."

Rayburn was an incorruptible politician. Under no circumstances would he be obligated to anyone; he would not even allow anyone to buy him a meal. At the time of his death he had no stocks or bonds and no significant savings; he owned only a ranch and some farm land that he had bought decades earlier. In the legislative halls in Washington, everyone knew that Sam Rayburn was "not for sale."

Born on January 6, 1882, in Roane County, Tennessee, the son of William Marion and Martha Rayburn, "Mr. Sam" had a normal upbringing in a rural American family that was honest and aspiring, if poor. When Sam Rayburn was five years old, the family moved to a forty-acre cotton farm in Fannin County, Texas, near Windom. They eventually adopted Bonham in northeast Texas, just a few miles away, as their permanent residence. After receiving his early education in a one-room schoolhouse, Rayburn attended Texas Normal College, now East Texas State University. He graduated two years

Press conferences on the House floor were rare, but Rep. Sam Rayburn called this one in January, 1947, when his term as Speaker of the House was interrupted and he accepted the Minority Leader's post. Courtesy of the Sam Rayburn Memorial Library, Bonham, Texas.

later with a Bachelor of Science degree. He taught in the public schools for two years before deciding that his talents were not for the classroom.

Partly under the influence of U.S. Senator Joseph Weldon Bailey, Rayburn began what was to be a distinguished political career. From 1907 to 1913 he served in the Texas House of Representatives and was elected Speaker during his last term. In 1912 he became the Democratic congressman from the Fourth District of Texas. The oath of office he took on April 7, 1913, initiated the longest continuous service of any member in the history of the House of Representatives, forty-eight years. He served as Majority Leader from 1937 to 1940, then was chosen Speaker in 1940 to fill the unexpired term of William B. Bankhead. For the next twenty-one years he served in this capacity, except during two Republican-controlled Congresses (1947–49 and 1953–55), when he was Minority Leader. In 1948, 1952, and 1956 he was also permanent chairman of the National Democratic Convention.

Rayburn was responsible for a great deal of important national legislation. In 1914 he introduced a measure that increased the power of the Interstate Commerce Commission, and in 1917 he sponsored the War Risk Insurance Act. During the period of the New Deal he authored the Truth-in-Securities Act, the Public Utility Holding Company Act, and an act establishing the Federal Communications Commission. Then, together with Senator George Norris of Nebraska, he secured the passage of the Rural Electrification Act. From 1941 to 1945 he fully supported the nation's war efforts. In the postwar years his leadership was crucial in passing President Harry S Truman's Fair Deal program and President Dwight D. Eisenhower's New Republicanism.

In 1949 Mr. Sam received the $10,000 Collier Award for distinguished service to the nation. As Speaker of the House for seventeen years (twice as long as Henry Clay, the previous record holder), Sam Rayburn displayed remarkable leadership abilities. His funeral in Bonham, Texas, was attended by political leaders from all over the world.

☆ This information on Sam Rayburn was supplied by Ben Procter, professor of history at Texas Christian University. If you would like to learn more about this national leader from Texas, you might read the biography by Charles Dwight Dorough, *Mr. Sam* (New York: Random House, 1962).

Tellin' Texas Tales

The tall tale is probably as much a part of the Texas image as the Alamo is. It is not just that Texans are known for bragging and exaggerating—they are—it is rather that the stuff of frontier life gives the material for good stories and the conditions of rural life give the time to tell them. So over the years Texas has developed a treasure trove of tales. Two of the best tellers of those tales were J. Frank Dobie and J. Mason Brewer.

Frank Dobie was the patron saint of the Texas Folklore Society and its leader for twenty years. For a third of a century he traveled through the state listening to its legends and tales. Then he wrote down these stories of the cowboy and the frontier, of mustangs and longhorns, of coyotes and rattlesnakes, and of lost gold mines and buried treasure that still haunt the children of Coronado.

Somewhere below Realitos there is a

139

well that still has six donkey loads of silver in it, according to one of Dobie's tales. Mexicans with the silver were attacked by bandits who killed the whole crew and made ready to take the treasure. The thieves, though, were set upon by gringos and killed—but not before they had thrown the silver, the Mexicans, and the donkeys down a well. One of the gringos found out about the silver in the well, so he bought the land and hired some Mexicans to clean the well out. When their digging struck bones the gringo told them to stop and he would do the rest.

"When the man got down there," Dobie tells it, "the first thing he did was to grab hold of a corner of an old *maleta* that he saw sticking out among the bones. He jerked it out and it had the dollars in it all right. Then he looked up and yelled to his helpers to pull. He hadn't more'n got the words out of his mouth when he saw a tall skeleton standing alongside the wall of that well. Its feet were close to him and it might have been twenty, maybe forty, feet tall. It reached clear up to the top, and its face away up there was looking down at the man. He couldn't take his eyes off it, and all the way up while those Mexicans were pulling him slow and jerky he had to look that skeleton in the face. He forgot all about that *maleta* of money and dropped it back, and when he climbed out he was so weak that they had to help him on his horse. They managed to get him home and put him to bed, and that night he died. And nobody that I know of has undertaken to get out those six jack loads of silver since."

Those six loads of silver are still there,

Texas folklorist J. Mason Brewer gathered stories in the Brazos Bottoms of East Texas in the 1920s and early 1930s, then worked with the Texas Folklore Society to publish them. By collecting these folktales from blacks only a generation away from slavery, he passed on language, customs, and religious forms that otherwise might have been lost or dramatically changed. ©Illustration by John T. Biggers for Dog Ghosts and Other Negro Folk Tales *by J. Mason Brewer (Austin: University of Texas Press, 1958).*

the Lost San Saba Mine is still lost, and treasure from the troves of Jean Lafitte and Santa Anna are still the stuff of the legends that Frank Dobie found and passed on to later Texas searchers.

Another premier teller of Texas tales was J. Mason Brewer, who became a leading American black folklorist. Brewer showed up at Frank Dobie's Texas Folklore Society office with a shoebox full of Negro tales that were later published under the title *Juneteenth*. Dobie, a keen and cutting critic, found the stories "genuine and delightful"; so the Texas Folklore Society published these tales and later ones as well. Brewer was a humorist and a satirist of the human condition. The black world of the Brazos bottoms that frequently served as his setting was the microcosm that mirrored mankind and the world.

While collecting preacher tales in the Brazos bottoms, Brewer ran across some anecdotes on snuff-dipping, an ancient habit. One tells of the Sunday that "Elduh" Waller preached a sermon entitled "Who Can Go to Heaven" and encountered some opposition in the congregation. The concluding dialogue, as Brewer records it, is an amusing comment on human nature. The preacher is in the midst of his strong sermon.

"He say, 'None of you liahs, you cain't git in.' 'Tell de truf!' shout Sistuh Flora. 'None of you gamblers, you cain't git in,' say de Elduh. 'Speak outen yo' soul!' squall Sistuh Flora. 'None of you whiskey drinkers, you cain't git in,' say Elduh Waller. 'Tell de truf!' shout Sistuh Flora. 'None of you snuff dippers,' say Elduh Waller, 'you cain't git in,' an' when he say dis heah, Sistuh Flora what got her mouf full of snuff rat den, jump up an' p'int her finguh in Elduh Waller's face an' say, 'Look ahere, Reverend, you've done stopped preaching and gone to meddling now.'"

The tales recorded by Dobie, Brewer, and others like them are an important link between the oral traditions and folkways of the past and contemporary Texas.

☆ The information on Dobie and Brewer comes from Francis E. Abernethy, who is present secretary and editor of the Texas Folklore Society, as well as professor of English at Stephen F. Austin State University. If you would like to read some of Dobie's works, you will have a good number to choose from, including paperback editions of *Coronado's Children, Tales of Old-Time Texas,* and *The Ben Lilly Legend,* published by the University of Texas Press. The same press published Brewer's *The World on the Brazos* in 1953.

Texas as a Western State

Once upon a time in Texas there were cattle drives. Everybody knows that. But the first cattle drives were not pointed north to Kansas, Nebraska, or Montana; they were pointed southeast to New Orleans. Before the Civil War many herds of cattle were driven from the Gulf Coast and East Texas to New Orleans markets. Yet in literature and film, the only cattle drives that existed are those epic journeys which took the cattle north along the legendary Chisholm Trail, the Western Trail, or the Goodnight-Loving Trail. This brief period of trail driving, lasting about twenty years, roughly from 1867 to 1888, laid the foundations for many legends, stories, poems, novels, songs, and movies about Texas, all of them committed to a western image of the state, all of them part of the process of cultural erasure that left East Texas and the Old South tradition far behind, as though they had never existed.

In literature the process of the westernization of Texas coincided closely with the rise of national interest in Western literature. For thirty years after the Civil War, dime novelists thrilled American youths with stories of Western buffalo hunters, outlaws, and intrepid frontier scouts. In 1902 Owen Wister published his highly influential romantic novel about the cowboy, *The Virginian,* and the very next year came an answer from Texas in the form of Andy Adams's nonfiction narrative, *The Log of a Cowboy.* Realistic, authentic, and well-written, Adams's book attained the status of a classic, but its depiction of the working cowboy's life could not compete with either Wister's glamorized cowboy or the romanticization of the Texas cowboy that would appear in that new art form on the horizon, the motion picture. *The Log of a Cowboy* was never made into a movie, but Emerson Hough's trail-driving novel *North of 36* was. In 1923 two of the chief defenders of Hough's novel against hostile Eastern criticism were men who were together going to do more than any other figures to align Texas with the Western rather than the Southern experience: J. Frank Dobie, folklorist, and Walter P. Webb, historian.

Dobie's successive collections of tales and legends, culminating in *The Longhorns* in 1941, found a ready national readership and made his Texas *the* Texas. His friend and academic colleague, Walter Prescott Webb, in *The Great Plains*

For writer J. Frank Dobie, the flavor of Texas was found in cattle drives, mining camps, and vaquero campfires. Dobie wrote scores of books and articles that typically defined Texas in Southwestern terms, though his own family came from southern stock. From The Longhorns *by J. Frank Dobie, illustrated by Tom Lea. Reprinted by permission of Little, Brown and Company, Inc. Courtesy of the University of Texas Press.*

(1931) lent enormous scholarly prestige to the image of Texas as a Western state. Like Dobie, Webb came down squarely on the side of vastness, aridity, cattle culture, and the view, traceable directly to historian Frederick Jackson Turner, that the American West was the true cradle of democracy. The Dobie-Webb scenario found many adherents among both scholars and writers. Zane Grey's novel *West of the*

Pecos (1931) opened in decadent post–Civil War East Texas, near the Louisiana border, but quickly launched the hero out west where his proper sphere of activity could be found: "Now he wanted to find the real Texas—the Texas that had fallen at the Alamo and that in the end had conquered Santa Anna, and was now reaching north and west, an empire in the making."

There was simply no way, apparently, that the old agrarian world of the South could compete with the man on horseback. Jay Hubbell, a literary scholar, wrote in the *Southwest Review* in 1924: "The Texas of the cotton farmer we still have with us. It is solid, honest, industrious, exploited, disgruntled, but, unfortunately, to the artist it is commonplace and dull." So much for East Texas and the Southern way. The allure of the cowboy over the sodbuster was so strong that even as gifted a writer as George Sessions Perry, author of the best Texas agrarian novel, *Hold Autumn in Your Hand* (1941), felt obliged finally to choose the cowman over the farmer as a mythic figure. Wrote Perry in *Texas, A World in Itself* (1943): "To us Texans there is a quality of go and glamour about cowmen that farmers never attain."

Movies reinforced and disseminated to millions, both here and abroad, the perception of Texas as a Western state. *The Texas Rangers, Texas, Red River*—these films and hundreds more from the late thirties on sealed the Western definition of Texas in the popular mind. Later, in the fifties and sixties, there were *Giant, The Big Country,* and *Hud.* Texas and the West became so firmly linked that when a Hollywood film departed from the stereotype, it did so with risk. *Return of the Texan* (1952), a gunfighter title if there ever was one, was actually a family picture about a man and his family returning to a Texas farm, but the title misled audiences and prompted studio head Darryl F. Zanuck to admonish the director, "When you go to Texas, go on a horse with a gun." Meaning: Texas was the wild West, not the settled agrarian South or Midwest. No farmers need apply.

After Dobie and Webb departed the scene, in the early 1960s, the Western tradition in Texas literature continued to flourish. Larry McMurtry is one major reason. His 1961 novel *Horseman, Pass By* was made into the famous movie *Hud,* and more recently McMurtry surprised everybody by publishing a monumentally long trail-drive novel, *Lonesome Dove,* which accomplished something none of his previous novels had been able to: suddenly McMurtry was number 5 on the *New York Times* Best Seller list. Working quietly in the shadow cast by McMurtry, older Texas novelists such as Benjamin Capps and Elmer Kelton have in the last three decades produced solidly researched and carefully crafted novels about West Texas past and present. Capps's *Trail to Ogallala* and *The White Man's Road* and Kelton's *The Time It Never Rained* and *The Good Old Boys* are in a way the fulfillment of Dobie's program for Texas literature.

In film the explosion of original Texas-based film projects, including *Tender Mercies, Terms of Endearment, Blood Simple,* has in no way eclipsed the national perception of Texas as a Western state. Films like *Urban Cowboy* and the long-running hit

143

television show "Dallas" have ensured the perpetuation of the century-long iconography of cowboys, oil, and macho values.

Dallas's legendary Southfork Ranch is a good index of the process of westernization. Located in Collin County, which was once part and parcel of Texas' Southern roots, a county whose economy was based on cotton farming, Southfork represents a stylized pseudo-ranch and the Ewings, who make their living plundering victims in the oil game — from corporate offices high atop Dallas, the most non-western of Texas cities — are presented in cowboy duds, boots, hats, and swaggering egos. The distinguished Texas novelist, William Humphrey, from far East Texas, said it best when he returned to his native Clarksville to collect impressions for his 1977 memoir, *Farther Off from Heaven*. Wrote Humphrey: "Red River County had ceased to be Old South and become Far West. I who for years had had to set my Northern friends straight by pointing out that I was a Southerner . . . found myself now in the Texas of legend and the popular image."

Civil Rights legislation, urbanization, and the presidency of Lyndon Johnson were all large factors in the displacement of East Texas and the Old South in the minds of natives and non-Texans alike. But the process could not have been accomplished without the image of Texas developed in the writings of Dobie, Webb, and Zane Grey and in the wholesale popularization of Texas' Western heritage in popular media ranging from picture postcards to stage plays, movies, and television. How long will the Western image of Texas last? Consider this sobering statistic: TV's "Dallas" enjoys widespread popularity in eighty countries, and there is no end in sight.

☆ Don Graham, professor of English at the University of Texas at Austin, wrote this perspective on Texas as a Western state. You can read more about the screen image of Texas in his book *Cowboys and Cadillacs: How Hollywood Looks at Texas* (Austin: Texas Monthly Press, 1983).

World War II

December 7, 1941, a Day of Infamy according to President Franklin D. Roosevelt, summoned Texans back to war. Like most Americans, they had endured the Depression of the 1930s as best they could and hoped that the United States would re-

main free from the wars that began in Europe and in Asia with the expansion of the Axis powers. But when war came, Texans, as usual, mustered.

News of the Japanese attack on American military installations in the Hawaiian

Texas not only sent thousands of its citizens to serve in the armed forces in World War II, but also provided training sites for many of the nation's military recruits. These trainees were lining up for a meal during training near Abilene in 1942. Courtesy of Alice E. Sackett and the University of Texas Institute of Texan Cultures, San Antonio.

Islands startled Texans, as it did other Americans, on an early winter Sunday. As they huddled around radios to learn more news, some were already determining to enter the armed forces to defend their country. Many had disapproved of the Burke-Wadsworth Act, creating the first peacetime military draft in the nation's history, when Congress had passed it in 1940.

Now they were willing to fight. Texas Senator Tom Connally, a member of the Foreign Relations Committee, introduced a declaration of war resolution in the U.S. Senate on December 8 and gave them a war.

Before long every branch of the armed services depended on training facilities in Texas. The Third Army, whose jurisdiction extended from Arizona to Florida, and

145

later the Fourth Army headquartered in San Antonio. Before war's end thirteen army bases within the state hosted soldiers. The Army Air Corps operated thirty-six training fields in Texas, including Brooks, Kelly, Lackland, and Randolph fields in San Antonio and others in Lubbock, Wichita Falls, San Angelo, San Marcos, Midland, and other Texas cities. Randolph Field, the West Point of the air, is the best-known air-training facility, but each field played an important role in preparing more than 200,000 aviators, gunners, and navigators for combat. The Navy also maintained facilities, at Corpus Christi and Grand Prairie. In all, more than a million service personnel received their military training in the state.

On the home front Texans had work to do. Aircraft plants, shipyards, and munitions plants provided jobs that were unavailable during the Depression. Civilians bought war bonds and savings stamps, accepted rationing of gasoline, sugar, coffee, shoes, and other items, and saved scrap paper and metals. In the absence of silk stockings, unavailable because the scarce material was used to make parachutes, women painted their legs with a liquid that resembled stockings when dry. They also went to work in all kinds of jobs, as more and more men enlisted or were drafted into the armed services. Children played "soldier" and helped adults tend "victory gardens." And over the course of the war, many a window displayed a black-bordered banner with a star, indicating that some serviceman or woman would not return to that home.

Texans fought in every theater of the war, but the Thirty-sixth Division, composed mostly of Texans and sometimes called the Texas Army, landed at Salerno, Italy, the first American troops on the continent. They fought for four hundred days in Italy, France, Germany, and Austria. More than twelve thousand Texas women served in the Army, Navy, Marines, Air Corps, or Coast Guard auxiliary services. The Women's Army Corps (WACS), commanded by Colonel Oveta Culp Hobby, herself a Texan, claimed the most women personnel, but Women Accepted for Volunteer Service (WAVES) and the other services also did their part for the war effort.

Texas produced heroes in keeping with its reputation: thirty-six Texans earned the Congressional Medal of Honor, and ten more the Navy's Medal of Honor. Texas also produced the most-decorated soldier of World War II. Audie Murphy, a five-foot, seven-inch, slightly built son of a tenant farmer from Hunt County, entered the army on his eighteenth birthday, after being turned down by the Marine Corps because he was too small. Murphy won a battlefield commission and every medal the army offered, including the Congressional Medal of Honor, as well as Belgian and French medals. His most famous accomplishment was in singlehandedly holding off a company of German infantry reinforced with six tanks by firing a machine gun from atop a burning tank after ordering his command to cover.

The most-decorated naval hero also came from Texas. Commander Samuel Dealey of Dallas, skipper of the submarine *Harder*, sank five Japanese destroyers within two days. After finishing off its last kill, the

Harder turned its belly up under water. Dealey regained control of the craft and managed to slip away to safety. He also was awarded the Medal of Honor.

Texas produced still other brave warriors. The first black hero of the war was a Texan. Doris (Dorie) Miller, a farm boy from the Waco area, was serving aboard the *Arizona* when the Japanese struck Pearl Harbor. Miller was a messman who worked in the ship's galley, and he had never had training or experience handling machine guns. Nonetheless, after fumbling several times with the loading device, he got one of the ship's guns loaded and managed to shoot down four Japanese aircraft. He did not leave his post until ordered to do so. For his outstanding bravery, he was awarded the Navy Cross. A hero's welcome and parade greeted him in both Waco and Dallas on a trip home, but he was lost at sea in November of 1943, when the *Liscome Bay* went down in the Pacific. His exploits were later commemorated by a recruiting poster issued by the U.S. Navy.

General of the Army Dwight D. Eisenhower, supreme commander of the Allied Forces in Europe, was born in Denison, Texas, although he moved with his family to Kansas when quite young. Admiral Chester Nimitz, commander-in-chief of U.S. operations in the Pacific, hailed from Fredericksburg.

In all, Texas sent more than 750,000 sons and daughters into the service of their country; 155 of that number became generals, and 12 became admirals. In every way Texas contributed heavily to the final victory.

☆ Information on Texas participation in the war was furnished by James W. Pohl, professor of history at Southwest Texas State University and director of the Texas State Historical Association. You can read the vivid account of one Texan's experience of war in the Philippines in *Bataan and Beyond: Memories of an American POW* by John S. Coleman, Jr. (College Station: Texas A&M University Press, 1978).

Katherine Anne Porter

Katherine Anne Porter once claimed to be "the first native of Texas in its whole history to be a professional writer. That is to say, one who had the vocation and practiced only that and lived by and for it all my life." She herself acknowledged that others had written interesting and valuable books about Texas, but she is probably the preeminent Texas fiction writer and the only Texas literary artist whose reputation is likely to survive into the twenty-first century. And it has been credibly argued that she achieved that status only because she left Texas.

Born Callie Russell Porter on May 15, 1890, in the Brown County community of Indian Creek, this daughter of an impoverished line of a distinguished Southern family absorbed from birth the rich lore of her region and of her poor but highly articulate and imaginative kin. "I am the grandchild of a lost war," she once wrote. Her mother died when Katherine was only two, and this Texas farm girl passed into the care and influence of her paternal grandmother, with whom the family went to live in Kyle, Texas, in Hays County. Her grandmother's character was a major factor in shaping Porter's personal development and served as the model for one of her most enduring fictional creations, Granny Weatherall of "Old Morality," "The Source," and "The Old Order." The farming communities of Central Texas, with their extended families, gothic race relations, and byzantine systems of social mores, also served as the setting of such of her stories as *Noon Wine,* "The Grave," and "The Circus."

The tradition in which Katherine Anne Porter—a name she appropriated from her grandmother—wrote, was not a Texas tradition. Stated simply, in 1920 there was no Texas tradition. Although a great number of novels, stories, plays, and poems—such as Amelia Barr's *Remember the Alamo,* Dorothy Scarborough's *The Wind,* and a goodly number of O. Henry's short stories —had been written during the first quarter of the twentieth century, the state had no internationally recognized literary figures and no corpus of critically accepted literary achievement. Katherine Anne Porter's literary community was, rather, the inter-

Best known by modern readers for her novel Ship of Fools, *Katherine Anne Porter wrote most evocatively about Texas experiences—and produced some of her best work—in early novellas and stories, such as* Pale Horse, Pale Rider *and* Flowering Judas. *Courtesy of Special Collections, University of Maryland Library, College Park.*

national republic of letters, and her closest associations were with the men and women who were chiefly responsible for the remarkable literary flowering of Kentucky and Tennessee in the 1920s and 1930s: the Fugitive and Agrarian writers and critics Allen Tate, Cleanth Brooks, Robert Penn Warren, and Caroline Gordon, who, like herself, spent much of their lives in self-imposed exile in the North or abroad. Also of great influence on Porter's life and art were Mississippians William Faulkner and Eudora Welty, her great friend.

Feeling herself "born to the practice of literature," Porter saw that she must leave her native state if she were to prosper in her craft. "I didn't know any genuinely working artists" in Texas, she said. "I think that it is because the South is a land of gentlemen, and gentlemen are patrons, not artists." She left Texas early, therefore, to follow her calling in Denver, Chicago, New York, Mexico, and Europe. Always, however, the small towns, the farms, and the history-haunted families of Central Texas followed her, forming the landscapes and populating the pages of her short story masterpieces. Even those stories and short novels set in other states or foreign countries most often deal with events in the lives of expatriate Texans, who range in type from the autobiographical Miranda Gay and Lieutenant Adam Barclay, the star-crossed lovers of *Pale Horse, Pale Rider,* to William Denny, the bigoted and obnoxious chemical engineer from Brownsville, in Porter's one full-scale novel, *Ship of Fools.*

In earlier days, Porter was sometimes slighted by her native state. A storm of controversy greeted the 1939 decision by the Texas Institute of Letters to give its award for best book of the year to J. Frank Dobie for *Apache Gold and Yaqui Silver* instead of Porter for *Pale Horse, Pale Rider.* Nonetheless, Porter's exquisitely crafted writing and inspired teaching have undoubtedly been a major influence on a new generation of Texas writers—her students William Humphrey, author of *The Ordways* and *Home from the Hill,* and William Goyen, author of *The House of Breath* and *Come, the Restorer,* perhaps best known among them. Although she returned to her home state only for brief visits or an occasional lecture from 1918 until her death in Silver Spring, Maryland, on September 18, 1980, Texas always remained for her "the native land of my heart."

☆ Material on Porter's literary career was provided by Thomas W. Cutrer, associate director of the Texas State Historical Association, and Marshall Terry, professor of English at Southern Methodist University. *The Collected Stories of Katherine Anne Porter* was published by Harcourt, Brace & World in 1970.

Urbanization

The shiny buildings of modern Houston or Dallas dwarf the old skyline of only a few decades past, and the city's sprawl has enveloped what was farm land only a few years ago. The force that brought this change—indeed, that changed the character of all American society—was the production demand of World War II. Before the war Texas and much of the nation continued in a rural and agricultural posture with the country's industrial services mainly centered in the urbanized Northeast. The war propelled Texas into the trend toward an industrial, urban, and technological society.

Texas' cities, especially Houston, Dallas,

Skyscrapers and highways like the Eastex Freeway indicated the accelerating urban growth in Houston following World War II. By the 1980s, three Texas cities—Dallas, Houston, and San Antonio—ranked among the ten most populous in the nation. Courtesy of the Houston Metropolitan Research Center, Houston Public Library.

Fort Worth, and San Antonio, were among those areas where these societal changes were most pronounced. The rapid urbanization that the war effort initiated in Texas continued almost unabated in the three decades that followed the war. The seeds of what is known today as the Sunbelt phenomenon had been sown.

In 1940, when the federal government decentralized the nation's defense establishment, new industries, such as aviation factories in Dallas and Fort Worth and shipyards on the Gulf Coast, were built in Texas.

Cities also felt the effects of the expansion of military bases, such as those in San Antonio. At the same time the fuel needs of the American war machine spawned a completely new petrochemical industry centered mainly on the Houston Ship Channel and in the Beaumont–Port Arthur area.

The end of the war brought the baby boom, igniting a true demographic explosion, and the economic forces the war had unleashed resulted in one of the most important population shifts in American history. Rural Texans had flocked to the cities to work in the new war-related businesses. For example, only 180 employees staffed the chemical industry in Houston in 1940; by 1949 the city had 20,000 chemical workers. The population of Houston nearly doubled during this period.

The pattern of rapid urbanization continued in the postwar years. The escalation of tensions in the Cold War perpetuated the wartime economy, to the benefit of Texas' cities. New industries continued to be organized, and firms began to relocate in Texas from the North. The Chance Vought Company, for example, transferred thirteen hundred employees to Dallas from Connecticut in 1948. In turn this spawned many auxiliary industries in the Dallas–Fort Worth region.

Increased construction began to change the physical appearance of Texas' major cities. New skyscrapers in Dallas and Houston dramatically altered their skylines. Work began in 1946 on Houston's massive Texas Medical Center, while a huge new business district took shape in the eastern section of downtown Dallas. A writer in Houston complained that "one is almost afraid to park one's car in a vacant lot for fear of returning to find it on top of a thirty story building which has sprung up in the afternoon."

The pattern of urbanization was influenced greatly by the expansion of the automobile industry and the parallel construction of the superhighway and freeway systems. The Gulf Freeway in Houston, the first in Texas, opened in 1952 and was soon followed by Dallas' Central Expressway. Freeways provided more mobility and radically altered the spatial configurations of Texas' cities as suburbanization – with suburban sprawl – soon dominated urban development. Houston, for example, grew in area from seventy-two square miles in 1940 to well over five hundred square miles by the 1970s.

The archetypical Texas suburb in the postwar years was Sharpstown on the southwestern edge of Houston. Sharpstown was the largest subdivision in the United States in the 1950s. Its ranch-style houses, shopping center, and residential streets feeding into a major freeway both symbolized and facilitated the life-style of the new urban Texas of the white middle class. It also provided a negative symbol, though – one of "white flight" as Texas' inner cities were increasingly abandoned to their growing populations of economically deprived black and Mexican-American citizens. By the 1950s, Texas was no longer predominantly rural. As late as 1940, half of all Texans had lived in non-urban settings; by the 1980s well over 90 percent of all Texans lived in cities.

The new urbanites of Texas viewed their cities in the postwar years with contradictory feelings of achievement and anxiety. As one writer observed on traveling through the booming Texas cities in the mid-1950s, many of the newcomers to urban life were "strangers, rootless in place and time." The urban centers of Texas, he mused, constituted an exciting but "nervous new civilization."

☆ This information comes from Don E. Carleton, director of the Barker Texas History Center at the University of Texas at Austin. He suggests for further reading R. M. Bernard and Bradley Rice, eds., *Sunbelt Cities: Politics and* *Growth since World War II* (Austin: University of Texas Press, 1983).

Separate, Not Equal

In the 1940s black Texans lacked equality in many ways, including the opportunity to obtain a professional education. Seated in the back of the bus, drinking from separate fountains, served from the back door of restaurants if served at all, and educated in separate and often substandard schools, they found little hope for change in their segregated life until after World War II. No matter how much the world changed, segregation seemed to go on forever.

During the days of slavery, Texans of African descent were rarely educated beyond what was necessary to do their assigned work. Education, it was correctly feared, would lead to freedom, at least freedom of the mind. In the aftermath of the American Civil War the Freedmen's Bureau and other relief agencies established schools that educated black adults and children at least in literacy skills. Most public and private schools were all white, including the state universities, and white Texans, like most whites in the states of the old Confederacy, accepted in principle the separate-but-equal doctrine established by the *Plessy* v. *Ferguson* decision in the 1890s as the proper way to educate the state's children. In practice, they accepted the "separate" more fully than the "equal" in that formulation.

Most school systems in Texas were in fact two systems, one for each race, at least in the areas where blacks were sufficiently numerous to justify them. The black schools were usually not as good, and in rural areas the school terms were not as long. One black joked, "It didn't take as long to educate us as it did you white folks; we only went to school for eight months a year and we usually got out a year earlier." Blacks who attended college, especially for graduate or professional degrees, had to travel to the West or the North, where they could gain admission, often with out-of-state scholarships.

The National Association for the Advancement of Colored People began to work for change in the segregation system early in the twentieth century. They successfully challenged the all-white Democratic primary election in the *Smith* v. *Allwright* case, then determined to desegregate the schools, beginning with the universities. They searched for nearly a year for a qualified black who would agree to attempt to enroll in a university as a test case. Heman Marion Sweatt, a Houston postal carrier who genuinely wanted to become a lawyer, agreed to try to enroll in the University of Texas Law School.

152

A Supreme Court decision in June, 1950, struck down University of Texas policies that prevented blacks from enrolling in its graduate schools. Heman Sweatt, the plaintiff in the NAACP's lawsuit against the university, registered for courses in the UT Law School soon after the decision. Courtesy of the Barker Texas History Center, the University of Texas at Austin.

When he was refused admission, he filed suit.

The Sweatt case was heard in the Austin court of Judge Roy Archer. Attorney General Price Daniel and assistants Jake Jacobson and Joe Greenhill represented the law school and the state, and Thurgood Marshall, James Nabrit, and W. J. Durham represented Sweatt. Before the trial convened, the state established a special law school for Sweatt in the basement of an office building near the state capitol in the hope that he would enroll or that the court would consider it a reasonable alternative for him.

It had no other students, and its faculty and facilities could hardly be considered equal to those of the University of Texas Law School. Nevertheless the state's lawyers attempted to argue that it was a separate-but-equal facility. And while the case was on appeal, the state established an entire university for blacks in Houston, which later became Texas Southern University.

Sweatt refused to accept either alternative. His attorneys argued that the facilities were not equal and that, in any event, segregation at all was inherently discriminatory, an argument that NAACP attorneys would use again in the landmark *Brown* v. *Board of Education of Topeka* case. The University of Texas administration held rigidly to its policy of excluding blacks, but many professors and students supported Sweatt. Some of them even organized a chapter of the NAACP on the segregated university campus.

The case was argued before the U.S. Supreme Court in April, 1950. Marshall presented Sweatt's case, arguing that the court should consider such factors as the law school's reputation and alumni status in considering whether the separate facility could provide Sweatt with an equal education and future career opportunities. When on June 5 the court ruled that Sweatt's exclusion was discriminatory, it established an important precedent for the desegregation of graduate and professional schools. Sweatt was admitted to the university amid great fanfare, and later other blacks challenged the remaining racial barriers on campus. Eventually all Texas schools, including public schools, were integrated, although often court orders were

153

necessary to force local school boards to do so.

⭐ Details on Heman Sweatt's case were supplied by Michael Gillette, chief of oral history at the Lyndon Baines Johnson Library, University of Texas at Austin. To learn more about the legal battles for desegregation, you could read the gripping account in Richard Kluger's *Simple Justice* (New York: Knopf, 1976).

Homegrown Rock

Popular music once meant folk music; in recent decades it has come to mean the music that appeals to the kid next door. Sometimes the music is even made by the kid next door, and on rare occasions that kid achieves a celebrity that lets him or her shape the way others make music. Two kids from right next door in Texas who have done that for rock music are Buddy Holly and Janis Joplin.

The roots of Texas rock go deep: to the ragtime rhythms of Scott Joplin, born near Texarkana; to the jazz trombone of Jack Teagarden; to the blues Blind Lemon Jefferson played in Dallas's Deep Ellum district; to the first commercial country music recording, in 1922, by Texan Eck Robertson. One of the hallmarks of Texas music has always been its open-mindedness, its willingness to borrow from other musical styles. The vibrant *norteña* music of Texas Mexicans along the Rio Grande shows the influence of the accordion polka music of Central Texas' Germans and Bohemians. Perhaps the best-known musical hybrid, though, is the unique style called Western Swing, especially the variety associated with Bob Wills. Wills was born in 1905 in East Texas, and when he began to play the fiddle, he admired the power and passion of black blues and jazz, both then popular. When he mixed them and played them on the stringed instruments of country music, he created an exciting, danceable, style called Western Swing that swept the Southwest and changed the country music scene.

Wills's Western Swing influenced young Elvis Presley, who in 1954 developed a related hybrid in Memphis known as rock'n'-roll. Elvis's early rock'n'roll—sometimes called "rockabilly"—strongly appealed to a young country performer from Lubbock named Buddy Holly. Although Holly died at the age of twenty-two in 1959, after only a few years of recording, he was one of the most influential figures in contemporary popular music. When the Beatles adopted American rock'n'roll, for instance, Buddy Holly and his group, the Crickets, were one of their major influences.

The exuberant, rebellious, and sexual nature of rock'n'roll disturbed the deceptively calm surface of the 1950s. Like Elvis, Buddy Holly captured the joyful, frantic energy of post–World War II youth in his

Buddy Holly and the Crickets from Lubbock emerged as rock-and-roll trendsetters in the 1950s. Holly's music and performing style influenced later rock-and-roll performers, including the Beatles. Courtesy of the Buddy Holly Memorial Society, Lubbock, Texas.

Janis Joplin moved from Port Arthur to Austin, then to California in the 1960s, taking along a distinctive blues singing talent and intense stage presence that captivated rock music audiences. Courtesy of CBS Records.

energetic sound and performance style. Unlike the often intimidating Presley, though, Holly had a nonthreatening, boyish, even childlike, image and style. With his friendly grin and horn-rim glasses, Buddy Holly personified the ordinary American teenager who had transformed himself into an extraordinary rock'n'roll hero. He symbolized the extravagant and exciting possibilities open to young Americans in the postwar era.

If Holly's significance derives in part from his accessible, "everyman" image, it is also based on his uncommon musical genius. An exciting guitarist and an adventuresome and distinctive vocalist, he wrote most of his own material, unlike many other early rock'n'roll heroes. He also developed an influential back-up band, the Crickets, whose instrumental lineup and sound became rock'n'roll standards. Buddy Holly became one of the most copied songwriters and stylists in the history of

155

rock'n'roll. When he died in an airplane crash in 1959, it was "the day the music died," as singer-songwriter Don McLean called it years later, although of course Buddy Holly's classic songs and image have endured.

Like all popular culture phenomena, rock'n'roll changed with the times, and a shy girl from Port Arthur named Janis Joplin expressed the tumultuous changes in the music and culture of the 1960s. Her passionate, blues-oriented style of rock music and her flamboyant dress and lifestyle made Joplin a national symbol of youthful energy and rebellion. In an era of musical and cultural revolution Janis Joplin was a defiant American individual who embodied the daring self-expression of the times. Although she was herself a sensitive, lonely young girl seeking acceptance and approval, she came to represent the personal "liberation" of a generation and the "new woman" rebelling against traditional standards of feminine beauty and sexuality. In life and death Janis Joplin reflected the complexities and contradic-

tions of the youth culture. Her generation's hedonistic, sometimes desperate, life-style was captured in her powerful, raging blues repertoire and uninhibited behavior. Her death from a heroin overdose in 1970 reflected her generation's searching, naïveté, and self-indulgence.

Buddy Holly and Janis Joplin humanized the rock music of their eras. They were major stars who grew up "next door," in Lubbock and Port Arthur, who were products as well as trendsetters, and perhaps victims, of their times. The indelible images and music of Buddy Holly and Janis Joplin have shaped the way we think and feel about those crucial decades in mid-twentieth-century America.

☆ This information was provided by George B. Ward, assistant to the director of the Texas State Historical Association and managing editor of the *Southwestern Historical Quarterly*. You can read more about these stars and their peers in *The Rolling Stone Illustrated History of Rock'n'Roll*.

The Johnson Legacy

Intimations of Lyndon B. Johnson's political potential appeared early, when he became the twenty-six-year-old state director of the Depression-era National Youth Administration for Texas. This early success hardly made him a national figure, but it focused the attention of national leaders on him as a young man to watch.

With his rise in the 1950s to positions as Minority Leader and then Majority Leader of the U.S. Senate, the youngest person ever to hold each of those posts, Johnson assumed national importance. He became active behind the scenes in destroying the influence of Senator Joseph McCarthy, and in 1957 Johnson reached

President Lyndon Johnson gave the Rev. Martin Luther King, Jr., a pen with which he had signed the historic Civil Rights Act of 1964. Courtesy of the Lyndon Baines Johnson Library, Austin.

the stature of statesman when he shepherded the first civil rights bill in more than three-quarters of a century through the Senate. Johnson insisted that if a civil rights bill was not passed then, another long era would ensue before Congress would have the courage to tackle the issue again.

Johnson's views on civil rights had been nationally known since 1949, when he had made it possible for a Mexican American named Felix Longoria, a posthumous recipient of the Medal of Honor from World War II, to be buried in Arlington Cemetery after a mortuary in Texas refused to receive his body. President John F. Kennedy appointed Vice-President Johnson to the President's Committee on Equal Employment Opportunity, a position that Johnson took seriously. He said, "It is my intention to sponsor any and every legitimate form of action that will produce results." Under Johnson's chairmanship the committee made progress toward ending discrimination by government contractors and government agencies.

When Johnson became president after Kennedy's assassination, he calmed the nation in its moment of fright and horror and then vigorously pushed his program through Congress, obtaining eighty-eight pieces of major legislation designed to improve the quality of life in America, along with hundreds of lesser acts addressing many large and small problems. Hardly a facet of political life was overlooked in the most active administration in American history. Among the results were the Inter-American Development Bank, the Kennedy Cultural Center, the Chamizal Convention ending a century-old dispute with Mexico, pesticide controls, the voting rights act of 1964, the War on Poverty, wilderness and recreation areas, food stamps, accelerated nursing training, library services, Medicare, Aid to Elementary Education, Aid to Higher Education, two new Cabinet-level departments (Transportation and Housing and Urban Development), highway beautification, arts and humanities foundations, air- and water-pollution controls, aid to small businesses, arms-control agreements, truth-in-packaging laws, safety programs, urban mass transit, new national parks (including Guadalupe and Padre Island in Texas), flexible interest rates, anti-age discrimination legislation, public broadcasting, the fair housing act of 1968, a bill of rights for Indians, Food for Peace, school breakfasts, truth-in-lending

provisions, aircraft noise abatement, guaranteed student loans, Redwoods National Park Service, protection against hazardous radiation, scenic rivers and trails, and North Cascades National Park. The list seems almost endless.

Many of the rules we live by now and the procedures that we take for granted as a people emerged under Johnson's leadership. To buy a house, purchase a used automobile, educate your child, treat your fellow citizen of whatever color or sex or age with respect, watch a tennis match live from Wimbledon—all of these activities have been influenced by policies promoted by Johnson, who had a Texan's belief that all things were possible if you put your mind to them. Moreover, he wanted to rid the world of inequities NOW.

Johnson's friends and foes alike will admit that involvement in Vietnam tarnished the otherwise bright record of Johnson's five and a half years in office. He escalated the conflict beyond the point that most Americans wanted to pursue it, yet would never go as far as the hawks wished. He thus faced criticism from both those who questioned whether American troops should be in Vietnam at all and those who thought the only reason you faced an enemy was to destroy it. These two camps of dissenters also, then, faced off against each other, contributing to a period of domestic social and political tension.

Some of Johnson's ambitious domestic programs have been refined by later presidents, some have been diminished, and since 1980 a considerable number have been dismantled. But no one has been able to ignore the cornucopia of social legislation that was enacted under Johnson's leadership. That much of it persists despite the fact that only one president from his own party has been elected since he left office dramatically shows how far he carried America during his administration. He is variously hailed as the Education President, the Civil Rights President, the Medicare President, and, of course, the Vietnam President, a title he shares with his successor, Richard M. Nixon. The imprint of Johnson on America remains a continuing factor decades after he left office.

☆ This overview of Lyndon Johnson's presidency comes from Joe B. Frantz, professor of history at Corpus Christi State University and professor emeritus of history at the University of Texas at Austin. If you want to know more about the significance of Johnson's career, you might read *LBJ and the American Dream* by Doris Kearns (New York: Harper and Row, 1976).

Sports and Society

Texans traditionally have honored sports and sporting events. Nowhere is this more evident than in their wholehearted embrace of high school football—in all parts of Texas, from the Golden Triangle to the smaller towns on the High Plains. High school football frequently involves the total participation of school and town in a ritualistic celebration of community. Cheerleaders, marching bands, and pep rallies all serve to intensify this ritual. Particularly in small Texas towns, the emotion of the football spectacle erupts in a crescendo of civic pride that helps define the boundaries of the community both geographically and psychologically. All ages and both sexes share in the sense of community that characterizes this experience.

The priority attached to the athletic experience at such Texas schools as Southern Methodist, Baylor, Abilene Christian, Prairie View, and Texas A&M (among others, of course) has fostered a kind of broader community among particular religious, ethnic, and even demographic groups within Texas. Furthermore, when a school represents Texas in an important intersectional contest, it usually enjoys the backing of the entire state. Intersectional rivalries such as the Texas–Oklahoma University game and the annual Cotton Bowl Classic have institutionalized opportunities for sectional pride. Begun in the midst of the Depression as an attempt to promote tourism, the Cotton Bowl has grown into one of America's premier college athletic events. Similarly, but to a lesser degree, the Dixie Series between the winner of the Texas League and the Southern Association once was a minor league baseball equivalent of the Cotton Bowl, providing fans of the Double A Texas League an opportunity to measure their heroes.

Sports have provided some minorites

159

an opportunity to gain recognition for their achievements and provide inspiration for young people. Texas has produced such outstanding black athletes that they were able to achieve fame even in the days of segregation. Rube Foster of Calvert, Texas, was an outstanding pitcher at the turn of the century. He virtually founded the Negro baseball leagues in 1920 and was eventually elected to the Baseball Hall of Fame in acknowledgment of his ability and leadership. Such illustrious players as Smokey Joe Williams and Willie Wells went from their Texas homes to baseball stardom in the big cities of the North. Later, Dallasite Ernie Banks made the transition from the segregated Negro Leagues to the Major Leagues look easy.

San Antonio's Ricardo Romo, running for the University of Texas, in 1966 became the first Texan and the first Hispanic to break the four-minute mile, making it in 3:58 minutes. And when Lee Trevino of El Paso won both the British and the United States opens in 1971, it was a significant breakthrough for the increasingly prominent Hispanic athlete.

Superstars Rogers Hornsby and Tris Speaker were among the first prominent southerners in baseball. "The Rajah," as second baseman Rogers Hornsby was nicknamed, had the best lifetime and single-season batting average in National League history. The .424 batting average he earned in 1924 is the highest in the twentieth century. Center fielder Tris Speaker, known for his blinding speed, helped revolutionize outfield play. He batted .300 or better during eighteen seasons, including ten in a row beginning in 1909.

Because Texas lacked major league baseball until the 1960s, college football challenged the national favorite, baseball, for the affection of Texans. Davey O'Brien of Texas Christian University became Texas' first Heisman Trophy winner in 1938. Other Texan winners included Doak Walker of Southern Methodist University and Earl Campbell of the University of Texas. Among professional football players, quarterbacks "Slinging Sammy" Baugh of the Washington Redskins and Bobby Layne of the Detroit Lions helped popularize the professional game and ultimately were elected to the professional Football Hall of Fame.

Between 1940 and 1948 Texans Ben Hogan, Byron Nelson, and Jimmy Demaret were the leading money winners on the PGA tour. Each won the Masters, golf's most prestigious tournament, as did Texan Ben Crenshaw later.

Mildred "Babe" Didricksen Zaharias was the star of the 1932 Olympics. She won gold medals for the hurdles and javelin and was awarded second in the high jump. She was also an extraordinary baseball and basketball player and won the United States Open Golf Championship in 1948, 1950, and 1954. She is often acclaimed as the finest female athlete of the century.

Texas was honored to have two Olympic track and field champions in 1956. Sprinter Bobby Morrow of Abilene Christian College was a double winner in the 100- and 200-meter dash, and Robert Richards repeated his earlier gold-medal performance in the pole vault. Randy Matson was a world record holder and Olympic champion in the shot put in 1968. In 1984 Carl Lewis of Houston won four gold medals,

The spectrum of outstanding Texas athletes has included Galveston's Jack Johnson, shown in his 1910 title bout with Jim Jeffries (top right; courtesy of William F. English, Austin, and the University of Texas Institute of Texan Cultures, San Antonio); Beaumont's Mildred "Babe" Didricksen, on the inside lane as she raced to an Olympic medal for the hurdles in 1932 (center right; courtesy of the Texas Sports Hall of Fame, Grand Prairie); El Paso's Lee Trevino, who captured the 1968 and 1971 U.S. Open golf tourney titles (above; courtesy of the Texas Sports Hall of Fame, Grand Prairie); and Tyler's Earl Campbell (bottom right; courtesy of the Austin American-Statesman), whose high school football performance led to a college record capped by the Heisman Trophy award, then a professional athletic career.

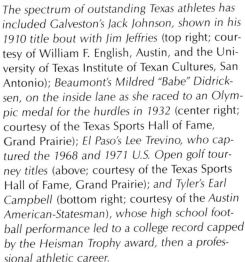

and Mary Lou Retton, who trained in Houston, reigned as the queen of women's gymnastics.

The importance of athletic prowess in Texas' culture is attested to by this string of honors, but it goes far beyond the holding of national championships to affect many aspects of life. The outcry met by the state legislature when it imposed "no pass—no play" requirements on the public schools in 1985 is perhaps another aspect of the same phenomenon.

⭐ Information on Texas sports heroes was provided by Donn Rogosin, lecturer in American studies at the University of Texas at Austin. If you are interested in the role of sports in society, you will no doubt enjoy reading *Sport Inside Out,* edited by David L. Vanderwerken and Spencer K. Wertz (Fort Worth: Texas Christian University Press, 1985), a delightful anthology of popular articles in which the sports analogy is applied to the individual, war, religion, death, and other facets of life.

Border Community

In the lower border area between the Nueces River and the Rio Grande a distinctive culture and life-style flourish. Although influenced by Anglo-Texan ways and words, it remains at its core border Mexican; its members call themselves Mexicanos.

The rituals—both sacred and secular—of this Mexican-descent community prescribe its cultural distinctiveness. Clearly showing their Hispanic roots, many border Catholics continue to make pilgrimages to a celebrated Catholic church in San Juan, Texas—pilgrimages that in some cases represent the fulfillment of another sacred ritual, the taking of a vow or *promesa.* In these contracts border Mexicans, particularly women, promise to carry out a form of self-denial such as giving extra prayer, cutting their hair very short, or making the long journey to San Juan if

some Catholic spiritual figure such as the Virgin of Guadalupe will assist them with one of life's many problems. In this way will a mother petition for the safe return of a teenage son from some mysterious far-away war.

Women may also enhance their communication with the spiritual realm through the artistic construction and ritual use of home altars to supplement the institutional church. Another sacred ritual that persists along the border, as in Mexico, is the visit to the *curadero(a)* or folk healer, when the patient believes that institutionalized medicine will not suffice.

A border ritual with both sacred and cultural significance is the *quinceniera,* the rite of passage of a fifteen-year-old girl into womanhood. In an elaborate church ceremony the girl's parents and her best girlfriends present her to God for His

The Virgen de Guadalupe, Mexico's patron saint, is an important cultural figure in Hispanic communities of the Texas-Mexican border region and in San Antonio, where Juan Hernández created this mural. Courtesy of Kathy Vargas, San Antonio.

blessing and protection for her coming years as a woman. Later in the day she is presented to society in a secular celebration complete with music, food, drink, and much dancing.

There is also a kind of semi-sacred ritual in the preparation and consumption of tamales, particularly during the Christmas season. The tamales, usually prepared by women working together, seem to symbolize the continuity of life itself, with the corn in *masa* (dough) form replaced in its husk to provide delicious nutrition. The cooperative preparation of the foods also affirms the bonds of female friendship and kinship, just as later the bonds of the family are affirmed as they consume the food. It is also customary to exchange dozens of tamales with other families in the *barrio* (neighborhood), so that before the Christmas season is over everyone has sampled everyone else's tamales and the larger community is affirmed.

Finally, the use of folk border Spanish, not to be confused with or called Tex-Mex, may combine the sacred and secular in a communal way. People may say to one who is speaking too much English in an all-Mexican context, *"¡Hablame en cristiano!"* (Speak to me in Christian!) —that is to say, not in the language of barbarians.

Language ritual also can have exclusively secular uses. For example, joke telling and speech play are highly valued forms of entertainment, particularly among men. The border community has a wide repertoire of complex forms of verbal humor that can be enjoyed in a variety of settings. One such setting is at weekend gatherings or the week-day *carne asada,* or barbecues, in which friends and family gather for the collective preparation and consumption of *fajitas, mollejas* (sweetbreads), *tripitas* (small milk intestines) with hot sauce, or beans and tortillas. This simple fare reaffirms the border people's linkage with their rural past, while at the same time strengthening social solidarity through the collective consumption of inexpensive food within the economic reach of a poor community (that is, before *fajitas* were "discovered").

Finally, there is the Texas-Mexican community dance, or *baile,* to the music of traditional *conjuntos* or modern orchestras, the ultimate secular ritual. On any weekend night and often during the week or on Sunday afternoon, working-class Mexican Americans in the Southwest, Midwest, and Northwest pay admission to enter the commercial, usually Mexican-American–owned, public halls to dance. In between dances they may momentarily sit in kinship or friendship groups at tables surrounding a large dance floor. They talk and drink beer purchased from concessions in the hall or from liquor bottles brought to the dance. However, during the three- to four-hour dance, most of their time will be spent on the dance floor.

They will dance in male-female couples to a Mexicanized polka that has "become something very close to a native folk form" in the twentieth century, according to Américo Paredes, a scholar on Mexican-American culture. While other dance forms such as slow-rhythm Mexican *boleros,* waltzes, Latin American *cumbias,* country-western, and rock'n'roll may be performed, the polka predominates. It is danced with the male leading his partner with a sliding step, their feet rarely leaving the floor, in a counterclockwise direction around the dance floor. This forward gliding motion is punctuated and elaborated with body dips and swinging turns, the latter probably borrowed from 1940s-era American swing dancing. Particularly skillful execution of all of these moves may occasion conversation and calls of approval from other dancers and from those sitting at their tables.

In its rituals, the border community expresses and solidifies its identity as a distinctive cultural enclave within Texas. Particularly in those which are communal in nature the Mexicanos find affirmation of belonging and meaning that transcend the social subordination implied by an Anglo-dominant society.

☆ This view of the border community came from José E. Limón, associate professor of anthropology at the University of Texas at Austin. You can read more about the region in Stanley R. Ross, *Views across the Border: The United States and Mexico* (Albuquerque: University of New Mexico Press, 1978).

Urban Cowboy

John Travolta on a mechanical bull, slugging down a longneck, or ramrod-still as he holds his partner in a Texas two-step, forms the image of the modern urban cowboy everywhere in the world. Perhaps it is just the pervasiveness of motion pictures that makes this so. But the world has been in love with Texas cowboys since they first captured the attention of the East in the first two decades following the Amer-

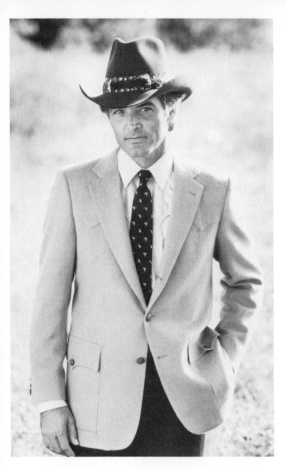

The fascination with the cowboy in the late 1970s and early 1980s is reflected in this 1981 fashion advertisement from Neiman-Marcus, which encouraged shoppers to adopt the "gentleman rancher's" attire. Courtesy of Neiman-Marcus.

ican Civil War. For at least a century the cowboy look, costume, music, life-style — everything that contributes to the myth — have been a source of identity to countless people who never saw a cow.

When the Texas cowboy rode into this myth he was mostly a hired man on horseback who borrowed his skills, equipment, and language from the Spanish vaqueros who had been working cattle on the range for centuries. Most of his trappings came from the *charro* culture that developed along the Rio Grande in the eighteenth century. By the time the Cattle Kingdom ended in America in the 1890s, the cowboy had captured the nation's imagination and had become the romantic embodiment of cherished American virtues. He had become a knight on horseback.

The cowboy's songs and exploits found an eager audience in eastern cities as early as the 1870s, when dime novels celebrating his kind began to appear. Soon cowboys appeared on the Broadway stage, in Buffalo Bill Cody's Wild West Show and dozens of imitators, and finally in motion pictures. The early Westerns of William Ince and William S. Porter formed for urban audiences the image of a self-reliant and usually victorious cowboy. Films with Tom Mix and William S. Hart in the 1920s enhanced the image, and Gene Autry, the personification of the "singing" cowboy, charmed audiences for a generation. Autry, from Tioga, Texas, gave the world an image of virtue in an elaborate costume later emulated by boys all over the country, even some who became real cowboys. It even became a kind of unofficial uniform for country music singers who headquartered far to the east in Nashville, but who toured the South and West to sing their songs in honky-tonks.

Modern urban cowboys swept America's cities in the 1970s, in a fad that took the music, dance, dress, pickup trucks, and values of the country to the streets, night clubs, and clothing stores of the city. This fascination with western ways developed at least in part because the cities themselves, rocked by a generation of dissent and protest, welcomed the traditional values and simpler ways of rural America.

Country music swept the nation, and rural dress, especially the cowboy variety, became fashionable. Beer joints and juke boxes invited friends—or strangers—to enjoy a longneck and dance the two-step or the Cotton-Eyed Joe. Broad-brimmed hats, plaid shirts with snaps, jeans, and boots abounded. But in the words of a Conway Twitty song, "Don't call him a cowboy until you've seen him ride." The minority of Americans who really did still live in the rural West, ride horses, and raise cattle for stock shows agreed with Twitty that boots and pickup trucks do not a cowboy make. The city dweller, said the redneck, was a masquerade, and within a few years he would move on to a new fad while the real cowboy kept dancing.

Perhaps part of the popularity of the urban cowboy was rooted in ambivalence toward the modern mechanical and technological age. The cowboy, the knight on horseback, was seen as his kind always has been: free, dominant, in charge of his life. His ancestors might have worked for wages, lived in bunk houses, and got wet every time it rained because there was no shelter out riding fence, yet he seemed to be free, singing "Don't Fence Me In" or, more recently, "Up against the Wall, Redneck Mother." The city dweller who spent his days at a desk made a great deal more money and wielded more power, but he did not feel free. So at Gilley's, in Houston, or at Billy Bob's, in Fort Worth, he took on the mechanical bull, a powerful symbol combining elements of the challenge of the Old West with the newer contest of man versus machine.

In characteristic fashion, modern humans confronted their problems in disguise. In this case the machine was disguised as an animal, a bucking bull. Using the popular image of the cowboy, individuals of the modern age metaphorically engaged in a competition with technology, employing an image of nature as a front for the act. And in characteristic fashion, people soon began to tire of that particular metaphor and moved on to new fads—California-style leisure wear or whatever—leaving the honkytonks again to the rural cowboy and perhaps his suburban son or daughter.

☆ Insights into the phenomenon of the urban cowboy were provided by Francis E. Abernethy, professor of English at Stephen F. Austin State University and secretary of the Texas Folklore Society, and Beverly Stoeltje, assistant professor of English at the University of Texas at Austin. You can pursue the subject in Jan Reid's *The Improbable Rise of Redneck Rock* (Heidelberg Publishers, 1974).

"Texan by Choice, Not by Chance"

During the 1970s, the media sold Americans on the good weather, jobs, and comfortable life-style that awaited them in the Sunbelt. For many people, Texas fit this

As immigrants and corporations streamed into the Sunbelt region in the 1970s and 1980s, the major Texas cities experienced rapid growth, spurring housing developments and roadways around their fringes. Courtesy of the City Planning Department, City of Fort Worth.

image to a tee. By 1980, one-third of the state's 14 million residents had been born somewhere else. If the 1970s' rate of growth continued, by the year 2000 one out of every twelve Americans would live in Texas.

In just the last five years of the decade, more than one and a half million people moved to Texas. This was not, as the popular image had it, just a matter of carloads of people leaving Detroit for Houston, though. Only 370,000 of these newcomers were from the Midwest. Another half-million came from the South, and 350,000 left a home in the West for life in the Lone Star State. Almost 90 percent of these migrants settled in heavily populated areas: 390,000 in the Houston-Galveston area, 350,000 in the Dallas–Fort Worth Metroplex, and 100,000 in metropolitan San Antonio.

Texas has also been a popular destination for foreign immigrants. Close to a million residents in 1980 were foreign-born, including a half-million from Mexico, 34,000 from Germany, and 25,000 from Vietnam. Not all of these foreign-born residents are citizens. Texas included 468,000 registered aliens in 1980, almost double the figure ten years earlier. Only California and New York claimed more registered aliens. There is no accurate count of the many thousands of additional aliens who are in Texas illegally. In 1980 the Border Patrol located 268,000 deportable aliens, 98 percent of whom were Mexican, and 3,500 of whom were from El Salvador. Most of these aliens were apprehended as they entered Texas, but monitoring hundreds of miles of border is difficult, especially since there are more than 100 million legal border crossing every year.

Newcomers, the birth rate of a relatively young population, and relocation within the state have had dramatic effects. The addition of 3 million residents during the 1970s won Texas three additional seats in the U.S. House of Representatives. Despite its frontier image and the fact that a majority of Texans lived in rural areas at the start of World War II, over 80 percent of the population now lives in the state's twenty-six metropolitan areas. Texas also boasts three of America's ten largest cities.

Absorbing this population growth has not been easy. State and local governments have been hard-pressed to provide more services, highways, mass transit, schools, and water. Often newcomers have faced hostility, including Ku Klux Klan denunciations of aliens. Housing has become more expensive and is often in short supply. Some recent migrants have even created "tent cities." Neighborhoods and communities frequently lack stability. Just over half of those living in Texas in 1975 were in the same house five years later. By the 1980s, growth itself had become a controversial issue, as Texas residents faced increasing pollution, congestion, taxes, and living costs. Neighborhood organizations, environmental groups, business leaders, land developers, and politicians have been involved in this debate, which will not go away as long as Texas remains an attractive place to move to.

Into the mid-1980s economic development kept pace with the rapid growth in population. During the 1970–80 decade, employment in energy-related businesses more than doubled; jobs were up in nondurable manufacturing, transportation and public utilities, wholesale and retail trade, finance, insurance, real estate, services, and federal, state, and local government. Manufacturing and services outgrew natural resources, energy, and agriculture, the historic roots for economic development in Texas.

Even though the national recession of the early 1980s affected all major sectors of the economy of Texas, most remained resilient and showed promise for continued growth. The positive Texas business environment accounts for past economic growth and diversification and will contribute to future growth. The absence of state corporate or personal income taxes, the presence of a stable work force, land and housing availability, a pleasant climate, and an entrepreneurial spirit are important factors in the business environment. Moves of corporate headquarters to Texas, like that of American Airlines, and plant expansions by major corporations can be directly traced to these factors. Most important, however, has been the creation of new businesses in Texas by Texans. The business enviroment has encouraged Texans to take entrepreneurial risks and build new businesses. In the five years from 1980 to 1985 the number of new businesses incorporated in the state averaged more than thirty-five thousand per year.

Looking ahead, the emergence of a recent trend holds great excitement and promise for the Texas economy: "high tech" has come to Texas. The Lone Star state now leads the nation in the number of high-technology firms created each year. In 1986 the state hosted more than two thousand manufacturing firms in nineteen high-technology sectors, including pharmaceuticals, office computing and accounting machines, electronic components, measuring and controlling instru-

ments, and guided missiles. This new era is expected to create jobs and provide income and opportunities for new business in Texas.

Still, neither the Sunbelt nor Texas alone is an economy unto itself. National trends and conditions will influence developments in Texas; the rapid growth itself could make the region less attractive. Perhaps it is appropriate to remember that the choice to move to Texas does not lay down instant roots; a choice can be reversed, and the bumpersticker "Texan by Choice, Not by Chance" can always be peeled off if the sun starts shining brighter in some other belt.

☆ Data on recent trends in Texas were provided by Victor L. Arnold, director of the Bureau of Business Research at the University of Texas at Austin, and Arnold Fleischmann, assistant professor of political science at the University of Georgia. The *Texas Humanist* for January-February, 1984, was devoted to a look at Texas cities under the influence of the Sunbelt phenomenon.

Murals as Community Art

Drab city walls have given way to brightly colored celebrations of a community's history and continuing identity in Mexican-American barrios (neighborhoods) throughout Texas. From San Antonio to Del Rio, Austin to Fort Worth, McAllen to El Paso,

vivid murals proclaim that the art of the people lives. These murals are not all alike in style or theme; they may grace the walls of the public housing units, neighborhood schools, and churches, or the office buildings and even supermarkets where the

The Community Cultural Arts Organization coordinated the design and painting of this outdoor mural on San Antonio's Westside. It celebrates the Spanish and Mexican Indian roots of the Mexican-American heritage. Courtesy of Community Cultural Arts Organization, San Antonio.

barrio does business. What they have in common is the community's interest and pride in its Mexican-American heritage.

Community murals are not new; they represent the revival of an art form that has been an integral part of the whole history and culture of the people of Mexico. Before the Spanish conquest of the Americas, the Aztecs and the Mayans documented the glories of their civilizations through murals. More recently, artists Diego Rivera, José Clemente Orozco, and David Alfaro Siqueiros used murals to promote the social and political ideals of the Mexican Revolution. Inspired by this artistic

tradition, many Mexican Americans have turned to murals for a creative outlet and to communicate their ideas to a broader audience.

The murals may be the creation of one talented individual or of an organization. A single artist, Raúl Valdez, has designed most of the murals of East Austin, for instance. Valdez spends a great deal of time talking with the residents of East Austin, who provide him with most of the ideas for his murals. Because they will have to see his murals every day, Valdez makes sure that the murals speak to the community and reflect the character of life there.

The barrio has enthusiastically received his murals, and he is never without volunteers to assist him with the painting. He has said that this participation by the community is as important as the finished art.

In San Antonio, on the other hand, it is a group, the Community Cultural Arts Organization (CCAO), that is responsible for the more than eighty murals located throughout the city's Westside. It was Anastacio Torres's dream in the late 1970s to put color and content to walls filled with ugly graffiti. Only one week after he painted a mural dedicated to the farmworkers at a housing project near his high school, he was astonished to find it spoiled by the work of graffiti vandals. Reasoning that a mural on private property might receive better care, he agreed to paint a mural on the back wall of a supermarket on the corner of Castroville Road and Cupples. When Torres showed a dozen teenagers that large blank wall one hot July morning, the mural movement got its start in San Antonio.

Unable to afford scaffolds to paint the upper parts of the twelve-foot-high mural, the artists stood on the roof of Torres's car. They plotted the design of the mural early each morning, then improvised as they went along. Torres painted some sections, but his crew looked to him primarily to organize the daily activities, which included keeping the paint cans filled. Color was not important; house paint and automobile paints were frequently mixed. The results, however, were impressive. The mural portrays the history of Mexico and the emergence of a Mexican-American people. The familiar motifs of Mexican culture—an erupting volcano, an eagle perched on a cactus, and an Aztec warrior—are prominently featured.

When the residents of the Cassiano Homes across the street took notice, Torres began the CCAO, a nonprofit organization dedicated to muralism, headquartered in the heart of the housing project. CCAO operates with a small staff funded by the city and with dozens of volunteers. The murals of Cassiano Homes have dramatically altered the cultural landscape of the community. The walls along Hamilton Street hold a powerful portrait of the Mexican revolutionary hero Francisco "Pancho" Villa, as well as a portrayal of Cleto Rodriguez, winner of a World War II Congressional Medal of Honor. Other murals in the district feature Bishop Flores, Christ on the Cross, Cesar Chavez, and the Virgin of Guadalupe. Sunset hues of red, purple, and blue predominate in the paintings.

While Torres continues to organize and raise funds for the CCAO, the group's creative work is now handled by Juan Hernández, an original member of the 1978 mural project. Hernández trains the neighborhood artists, some as young as ten years old, to sketch and paint. He also oversees conservation efforts, an increasingly important task now that some of the murals have been around several years. As from the beginning, from the time the scaffoldings are set up and the paint cans opened, the community is involved: the elderly come to watch and to talk to the muralists; the children and teenagers help with the painting. Once the mural is completed, all the residents are invited to participate in the celebration.

Most Mexican-American muralists, then, are not artists in the professional sense. Very few of them have had artistic training, and even fewer have contemplated careers in art. Most of their materials are donated, and they work for no pay. The muralists paint for a variety of reasons, but they all share a commitment to their community that enables them to bear with all the discomforts muralism entails. After all, if it is difficult to paint a large canvas inside a studio, the difficulty multiplies when the artist works with the distractions of city noise and under a hot sun.

The interests and concerns of these muralists—and their communities—vary. Many walls deal with cultural themes: the family, education, religion, heroes, holidays, and celebrations. Others have historical themes: Aztec civilization, the U.S. War with Mexico, the Vietnam War. Historical murals generally reinterpret history from a Mexican-American point of view.

One of the most important elements of Mexican-American muralism is that it is public art. Wall art is not something cold and abstract, stuck away in an elite gallery or museum, but something that reflects the lives and experience of the common people. The community can take pride in its museum without walls. The active role the neighbors play in the creation of this artwork is important. Without this public base of support a mural cannot "live" in a community; it is alien and out of place. But a mural that is accepted, that captures the concerns or the dreams of the people who live there, does more than symbolize their culture; it affirms and strengthens their very being as a people.

☆ The information on mural art comes from Maria Cristina García, assistant instructor in American civilization at the University of Texas at Austin. Ricardo Romo, associate professor of history at the University of Texas at Austin, furnished information on the CCAO. You can view Mexican-American murals in many Texas cities; the Mexican American Cultural Center in northwest San Antonio arranges for minibus tours of that community's mural art.

Folklife Festivals

Every August Texans from around the state gather in San Antonio to celebrate the diverse roots of their common identity. The Texas Folklife Festival, hosted by the Institute of Texan Cultures, is the state's biggest ethnic festival. It is a tribute to the rich cultures of the many ethnic groups—black, Jewish, Polish, Mexican, Korean, Spanish, more than thirty groups in all—who settled Texas and made the blend of their cultures Texas culture.

Each group displays its distinctive music and dancing, its arts and crafts, its traditional work ways and life-styles. In festive booths arrayed on the grounds, the various groups sell typical foods. The Japanese offer teriyaki and yakitori, the Jews sell bagels and potato knish, and the Poles sell pierogi, stuffed dumplings.

The several stages set up at the Festival feature the music and dances of the diverse groups represented. One stage spotlights Anglo country-and-western music; another, Mexican folk dancing and mariachis. Scottish bagpipe bands parade regularly through the grounds, and Filipino tinikling dancers perform rhythmic steps over moving bamboo sticks.

Festival visitors can play traditional games, such as the Italians' *bocce* and Belgian *bolls*. They are invited to watch potters at their wheels and wood carvers and rope plaiters at work and to observe construction techniques on traditional log structures.

Ironically, the very nature of a folklife festival's planned and organized celebration of a multi-ethnic past is also a reminder that these roots *are* a thing of the past; the festival does not spring spontaneously from daily life, but must be carefully orchestrated in a deliberate re-creation. At the folklife festival, visitors are, in an important sense, tourists in the cultural past, spectators at performances of staged authenticity, observers of re-creations of folkways, not participants in the folkways. Moreover, people attend these festivals not so much to enjoy their own cultural traditions as to be entertained by the cultures of others.

To be sure, there are still local festivals in some parts of Texas that do represent a particular community's celebration of its identity and the aspects of life that embody it. A community may celebrate its

Texans of Filipino descent share a traditional dance with visitors at the Texas Folklife Festival in San Antonio. Music, dance, and food are the chief features of this annual festival. Courtesy of the Texas Folklife Festival, University of Texas Institute of Texan Cultures, San Antonio.

major crop at the time of harvest, as Poteet does in its Strawberry Festival or Luling in its Watermelon Thump. It may feature a distinctive aspect of its environment, its culture, its history, or its seasonal pastimes. Woodville celebrates the blooming of the dogwoods in its forests with a festival; Tyler, the blooming of its acres of cultivated roses. Hamilton's Dove Festival each year opens the hunting season, important not only economically but also culturally in this rural community. Old Settlers reunions, Old-Time Fiddlers contests, and Bluegrass Music festivals abound in Texas to commemorate the founding or perpetuate the folkways of a community.

The festival might, on the other hand,

173

celebrate a community's dominant occupation; for example, the rodeo at Stamford's Cowboy Reunion celebrates the ranch life of West Texas, and the Blessing of the Fleet commissions Port Lavaca's shrimpers for another season. Then, too, there are local ethnic festivals that display the distinctive roots of a town or county. The Czechs of Ennis have a Polka Festival; the Germans of New Braunfels, a Wurstfest; the Norwegians of Cranfills Gap, a Lutefesk; and the Mexicans of Brownsville, Charro Days.

These local festivals are more traditional than the Texas Folklife Festival in San Antonio. In them, the people put their culture on display, for themselves and for others. Their festivals are rooted in an established sense of community, and they employ a range of symbols to build festivity: food, drink, music, dance, color, costume, and so on. Yet in these celebrations, too, what is put on display is precisely what modern, urban, industrial life is distancing the communities from: their agrarian and ethnic past in folk society. In modern Texas traditional folklife is seen as at least endangered if not a thing of the past. It may be regarded as attractive in a nostalgic way, but it is seen as no longer fully viable. What the festival—community-based tradition or multi-ethnic, sponsored event—does do is reaffirm ethnicity, celebrate particular cultures, and offset the negative views of the traditional, the rural, and the ethnic that have been fostered so strongly by the American ideologies of progress through technology and homogenization in the melting pot.

Rather than being rooted in an established sense of community, as the traditional festival was, the folklife festival represents an attempt to create a sense of community, to foster the notion that we do have something in common despite the ethnic, regional, and historical diversity and social differentiation that mark our background as Texans. What we have in common, though, turns out to be—perhaps—our distance from our traditional past.

☆ This information was provided by Francis E. Abernethy, professor of English at Stephen F. Austin State University and secretary of the Texas Folklore Society, and Richard Bauman, professor of anthropology at the University of Texas at Austin. The Texas Folklife Festival takes place each year the first weekend in August; if you would like to attend, you can get tickets in advance or at the gate.

Texas Architecture

From highly portable wigwams and temporary log cabins to high-tech, glass-skinned skyscrapers, Texas architecture has embodied mobility, flexibility, and the ability to adapt the land to human purposes.

The first nomadic Indians lived in port-

Bottom right: *Texas Indians and Franciscan friars collaborated in the design of living and working quarters in Mission San José y San Miguel de Aguayo near San Antonio de Béxar in the eighteenth century.* Courtesy of the Texas Highway Department, Austin. Top right: *Andrew Smyth of Jasper County, a soldier and shipper, built his 1849 home in the traditional dogtrot style. The middle passageway was closed in by a later owner.* Courtesy of the National Register Division, the Texas Historical Commission, Austin. Above: *The spare post-modern forms of corporate office buildings contrast with the Gothic Revival details in this Methodist church built in downtown Dallas in 1926.* Courtesy of First United Methodist Church, Dallas.

able tipis, while sedentary tribes lived in dwellings that were stationary, if fragile. Early explorers in Texas discovered Patarabueye and Jumano villages consisting of clusters of low, flat-roofed rectangular buildings with walls of palings and adobe along the Rio Grande. In East Texas, the Caddo Indians erected circular houses perhaps fifty feet in diameter with conical roofs made of frameworks of rafters and purlins tied together and thatched with bundles of grass. Between A.D. 1200 and 1500, Indians in the Panhandle near the Canadian River used materials at hand to build durable, pueblo houses with stone walls and flat roofs. But they had vacated these houses by the time the Europeans arrived.

During the European settlement of the region of Texas, each ethnic group transplanted its traditions and values, including building techniques and styles. With cross and sword in hand, Spanish colonists journeyed into the northernmost wilderness of New Spain to convert the natives. As part of this process, they constructed handsome and durable churches in the architectural style of Spain, and they erected forts, called *presidios,* whose severe lines advertised the military presence. During the Spanish and Mexican eras, *casas grandes* (large houses) fortified with thick stone walls reflected the architectural forms of the ranchers' homeland and provided security against the warring Indians who roamed the area along the Rio Grande.

A variety of building types dating from the nineteenth century reflect the lifestyles and customs of a potpourri of cultures emanating from several European countries. Houses with *fachwerk* (halftimber) walls remind us of the German presence; houses with *palisado* (vertical pickets) walls attest to French and Hispanic settlement; log cabins with breezeways evoke memories of Anglo-American architecture in a hot climate.

As soon as possible, Anglo settlers replaced these rude log cabins with more imposing structures. Colonnades of the Doric or Ionic order became emblems of eastern taste and refinement, as well as a symbolic identification of Texas with Greece, the cradle of democracy. Gothic churches, epitomized by pointed arches,

attempted to associate the nineteenth century with the earlier age of faith. County courthouses, prominently located in the town square, stood as symbols of democratic government; the bells in their cupolas sounded alarms and regulated the community's activities.

The economic surge following the Civil War financed a flood of gingerbread, spindlework, turrets, and a host of other picturesque features on Victorian houses. New technologies led to the mass production of building components and to such newfangled features as electrical lighting, electric street cars, and running water. This era of overstuffed elegance eventually gave way to a period of more disciplined Classical splendor. Seeming to reflect the imperial ambitions of the country, large buildings with ranges of Greek or Roman columns served as palatial residences, churches, art galleries, libraries, and government edifices. In the 1920s and early 1930s, the "moderne" look took hold; whether dazzling art deco or shining and streamlined, the look was untraditional and decidedly novel. At the same time, Texas architects such as O'Neill Ford sought to revive the traditions of the Texas ranch house and the Spanish *boreda* domes in residential architecture. The Great Depression of the 1930s brought this period to a close. Hard times are suggested by the stripping away of ornamental features, leaving boxlike forms. Assisted in many cases by President Franklin D. Roosevelt's New Deal programs, numerous public buildings appeared, barren of ornamental features.

Following World War II, corporate America embraced the "international style," and suddenly glass "curtain" walls and seemingly weightless white boxes were the new symbols of modernity. This minimalist attitude has recently given way to a reserved appreciation, albeit sometimes ironic, of historical styles. The traditional and the modern exist side by side and await the next developments in Texas.

☆ Willard B. Robinson, professor of architecture at Texas Tech University, supplied information for this overview of Texas building styles. For a fascinating pictorial survey of Texas' architectural history, see Professor Robinson's book *Gone from Texas: Our Lost Architectural Heritage* (College Station: Texas A&M University Press, 1981).

The Texas Mystique

Until Alaska entered the Union, Texas was unique among the United States by virtue of its size. In mythic terms, Texas is still the biggest state. It is the only state that has a separate identity known equally in Great Britain, Germany, Peru, and Zimbabwe. The Texas mystique, which is as good a name as any to call this phenomenon, can be defined visually and aurally. The stereotypical Texan is a larger-than-life figure of bluster, power, and crude energy. He talks with a heavy drawl and has a costume as recognizable as an Arab sheik's: hat, boots, string tie, and big belt buckle. His favorite song is "The Yellow Rose of Texas," his favorite drink is bourbon and branch water, and his favorite automobile is the Cadillac. He is polite to women and likes to call them fillies. He loves the Lone Star State, the Dallas Cowboys, and America, in that order.

This stereotype, which has a long and colorful history in American popular culture, has been disseminated in many media, including plays, dime novels, penny postcards, Western pulp fiction, country and western music, and of course motion pictures and television. But the stereotype has been perpetuated also in more serious forms of discourse. Without Texan historians, for example, it might never have achieved such long-lived currency. The Texas Rangers, in Walter P. Webb's words, "rode straight up to death," and most accounts of the Alamo bear stirring witness, movie-prologue-style, to the equation of this battle with the greatest known in history.

In truth, early Texas history laid the groundwork for later myth-making. Three signal events formed the basis for the creation of the Texas mystique: the long-term existence of the Texas Rangers and their immense popularity as figures of frontier justice; the Alamo and the titanic figures associated with it and with the creation of the Republic of Texas, men such as Davy Crockett and Sam Houston; and the cattle

177

George Stevens's 1956 production of Giant *for Warner Brothers Pictures added the film image of the oilman to that of the Texas rancher or cowboy. James Dean played the role of an oilfield roughneck. Courtesy of the Museum of Modern Art, Film Stills Archive, New York.*

drives following the American Civil War, the greatest epic expression of the generic American hero, the cowboy. Such historical phenomena stimulated the imagination of hundreds of novelists, poets, and dramatists, and by the beginning of the twentieth century, as the movies came into being, there lay at hand a vast reposi-

tory of history and romance from which stories for the newest mass medium could be devised. Charles Hoyt's popular stage farce of the 1890s, *A Texas Steer*, was filmed twice, and the stories of Zane Grey that were set in Texas were filmed even more often.

To add to the nineteenth-century legacy

of history and frontier destiny, Texas in the twentieth century became the richest oil-producing state in the nation. To the rancher-cowboy stereotype was thus added the oilman, or the wheeler-dealer, and in movies such as *Giant,* both traditions received their full due. From them Texas acquired further definition as a lusty frontier state full of raw vitality and primitive American values. After the assassination of President John F. Kennedy in Dallas in 1963, the Texas mystique underwent a significant negative revision, and all the latent, darker implications of the old frontier were then given full play, as sinister and corrupt. The Texan was portrayed as a right-wing extremist.

Then, in the late 1970s, the Texan was transformed once more into an attractive protagonist in such vehicles as the television show "Dallas," which proved popular in eighty countries around the world, and in *Urban Cowboy,* which redeemed the redneck from a decade of scorn. The high watermark of Texas Chic—a blend of fashion, hyperbole, and hype that left half the country owning a pair of boots and a hat decorated with plumage from an endangered species—was achieved in 1980. During the Sesquicentennial celebration the Texan of myth and popular culture is once more in the limelight, where he has been so many times. From Davy Crockett and Sam Houston to Tom Mix and J. R. Ewing, the Texan has proven one of the most elastic and enduring of our national icons.

☆ Don Graham, professor of English at the University of Texas at Austin, wrote these reflections on the Texas mystique. You can read more about the myth and reality of the Lone Star state in *Texas Myths,* edited by Robert F. O'Connor and published for the Texas Committee for the Humanities by Texas A&M University Press in 1986. This subject is one that all Texans experience themselves; so you can also learn more about it by talking with people about Texas and, if you are Texan, by living more attentively.

The Texas Experience has been composed on the Compugraphic digital phototypesetter in ten-point Optima with two points of spacing between the lines. Display type was furnished from the same type font.

The book was designed by Jim Billingsley, composed by Metricomp, Inc., Grundy Center, Iowa, printed offset by Thomson-Shore, Inc., Dexter, Michigan, and bound by John H. Dekker & Sons, Grand Rapids, Michigan.

The book is printed on acid-free paper designed for an effective life of at least 300 years.

 TEXAS A&M UNIVERSITY PRESS : COLLEGE STATION